Me and Danny

Growing Up in Small Town America

Michael Cerza

Dedication

This little volume is humbly dedicated to best friends everywhere, especially those of us whose minds sometimes wander over to considerations about such lofty things as the elasticity of time, who find it curious as to why the hours seem to fly by when we're at a particularly awesome party or on a long-awaited vacation yet drag like crazy at the dentist.

Could it be that the escapades of a long-ago time are nearer than we think?

Acknowledgements

I wish to thank my mother, Antoinette; my dad, Frank; my brothers, Robert, Paul, and Felix; and my sister, Fran. I also want to thank my children, Erica and Zack; my former spouse, Barbara; my wife and editor, Kristie; and all my friends. For without you--all of you--I would not be who I am today.

And of course, my friend Danny and his big brother, Charlie wherever they are.

Author's note: Although all the events in this story are true, some of the details might be a little sketchy, owing to the decades that have passed. Also, some of the names have been changed to protect the innocent…you know who you are.

Introduction

Many years ago, I had a best friend. His name was Danny—Danny Wiggins— and he lived a few streets from my back door. If I cut cross-lots behind my house, I could be there in two minutes flat. The town in which we lived is still there. It's called Seneca Falls and it lies in upstate New York, kind of halfway between Syracuse and Rochester. The name was always a bit of a mystery; some said it was named after a great Native American who, legend has it, fell from a high precipice somewhere nearby. Personally, I hope this isn't the case. I figure they've suffered enough already without making it any worse for supposing. Another idea, perhaps more historically accurate, was that there was once a tiny falls in the middle of the main waterway that flows through the village. I like this one because it paints such a quaint picture of our little town in a time long before this time.

Me and Danny

Back then the village of Seneca Falls was pretty small; not even enough of a population to be called a town much less a city. Seemed everyone either knew each other or knew why they didn't want to. It was a lovely little place tucked away in a part of the country that didn't know much about the rest of the bigger world that surrounded it. But what it lacked in the way of big city diversions it made up for in the many ways for us kids to amuse ourselves.

Like other kids our age Danny and I just screwed around doing whatever we could do to have fun. We played basketball by the hour in his cement driveway, passing the ball back and forth, tossing up brick after brick, heckling each other the whole time. Of course, Danny, being much taller and a little beefier than I, could have easily rolled right over me if he wanted to—me all of 90 lbs. soaking wet.

On rainy days—days that were so long they seemed to stretch into two—you'd find the two of us on Danny's front porch brushing acrylic paint onto our newest "action figure Superhero" model, jawing back and forth about who would win in a fight, The Hulk or The Silver Surfer, Superman or The Green Lantern. We never discussed anything too serious; I mean we were only 10. Not that we didn't have our little spats mind you. And it seems they always took place in the heat of summer.

Heat…In upstate New York? In a town barely a half days' drive from the Canadian border? Surprising, I admit. But let me tell you…sometimes—especially during particularly long stretches of hazy, humid days—it was so stiflingly hot my brothers and I would beg Dad to turn on the fan of the ancient furnace down in the cellar, just to get some cool air. The air was cool all right but damp too, coming up from that dimly lit stone and dirt-floor cellar. The only people who had central AC back then didn't live in our part of town, if you know what I mean. But even with the cellar fan, by the fourth or fifth hot-as-blazes day in a row—we'd all want to just go jump in the lake—literally.

Me and Danny

But did we have a lake? Oh my, did we ever! Cayuga Lake, an amazing body of water—some 45 miles long and 400 feet deep—is a huge clean freshwater oasis! In addition to its crazy-large size, it also has a rather unusual attribute: its shoreline. At water's edge—where you'd expect to find sand or rocks—there are thousands and thousands of gray stones. What's the big deal about stones around a lake? Well, they were all flat; not just some of them, all of them, like a zillion little grey pancakes. Turns out this was the work of prehistoric ice cubes the size of Texas that rolled through the area cutting deep grooves in the earth as they went…or so my Dad used to tell me.

Now what made these stone pancakes so special was the game we played with them. We picked them up and tossed them into the water. What's the big deal with that? Well, it's true all we did was throw them; remember this was 1962, before devices with tiny buttons and bright screens. But we didn't just pick them up and wing them toward the lake. We played a little game with them, a silly, friendly little game but one with a clear winner and loser.

If you wanted to win, you'd have to learn the proper technique. There was a trick to it. You had to grip the little stone pancake in such a way as to allow it to be tossed low and absolutely parallel to the surface of the water. The idea was to make the thing skip across the top—just barely kissing the surface. This made the stone ride along its spinning flat edge, ricocheting off the surface as it went. That was it; that was the game. Seeing who could skip these stone pancakes the most times before finally splunking in, 1,2,3,4,5,6,7 times. It was just easy fun for Dad and me, my brothers and sister on family picnics and sometimes Danny and me—when we were lucky enough to go to the lake. Cool, right? Well, as I said, those were simpler times.

Anyway, when it got hot and humid like that, Danny and I naturally sought relief, hence the trip to the lake. The trouble was that Cayuga lake wasn't in walking or biking

Me and Danny

distance, so we had to have a ride and for this, we were pretty much dependent on Dan's mother. This was because my Dad was at work and my mom never took us anywhere, seeing as how she had 5 kids to take care of and we only had one car that worked. Of course, there was Dan's Dad but he was just too old to even stand up. I swear in the all the years I knew Dan, I never saw the guy on his feet; he was always sitting in an easy chair in the front room of the house with his big old nose in a big-old book.

In any event, when it came time to get out of the heat, it always came down to me convincing Dan to bug his mom. I say bug because his mom was kinda on the old side and would just as soon stay home. She wasn't mean or anything. In fact, when she did take us down the lake, she didn't just take us down to where everyone else went, the overcrowded Cayuga Lake State Park pavilion, with its over-priced concession stand, stale candy, and damp popcorn. I mean it was cool and all but that cold slate floor—that got

6

really slick when wet, which it always was—seemed to bring out a certain smell...something between a mildewed shower curtain and an ear of sweet corn.

Yeah, looking back on it, I have to admit that it was pretty nice of her to chauffeur Danny and his best friend to the lake just so they could cool off. The place she took us to was right on Route 89, the road that parallels the lake. All she had to do was turn off and park. And there it was, a little stretch of stone beach that gave us direct access to the crystal-clear water of Cayuga Lake. And no one was ever there so we had the whole place to ourselves.

In addition to being a nice lady, Danny's mom was a nurse too; in fact she was the one who taught me to dry my hair first after swimming. She said this was because you lost most of your body's heat from your head. And of course this was great advice because when Danny and I got out of that 60-degree lake water, we sure wanted to get warmed up as soon as possible!

7

Me and Danny

Anyhow, when things got unbearable in town, approaching Danny's mom was our ticket to relief. This one time...

Saturdays

Looking back across these six decades it feels like the sun was always shining. But I guess this is just my selective memory; it did rain occasionally of course. And on these rainy days my best friend and I would break out the acrylic paints and that nasty, brain-eating glue—that smelled so good. Hour after dreamy hour Danny and I would work on our models. I remember the dark gray sky, the lazy sound of rain on the wide porch windows, the cool damp summer air, the idle chatter. Good stuff. This one time...

Dan and I were on his front porch—one of those enclosed deals where it was originally just a porch open to the air then walls and windows put in to stop the bugs in the summer and the cold in the winter. It was a Saturday

9

Me and Danny

morning; we'd already finished watching our favorite cartoons and were fixing to shoot some baskets. The weather had other plans. As we ran out the back door toward the driveway, the skies opened up. It was raining hard now. Plan B: out came our models and our paints and before you could say George Jetson, we were brushing fresh paint onto our most recent action figures: Hulk for him, Superman for me.

"So d'you think your mom's gonna take us swimming, or not?" …

Silence.

"Dja' hear me?"

"What?"

"I said, are we goin' swimming tomorrow or not? I gotta know cuz I need to ask my mom if it's ok.

"OK to do what?" Dan asked without looking up.

"To go swimming, for the millionth time!"

"Well is she?"

"Is who?"

"Your mom....is she gonna take us swimming?, Jeez Dan watsa matter with you?"

"Me, nothing...why?"

"Never mind!"

"Never mind what?...What did you say for cryin' out loud?"

" I just wanted to know if you asked your mom yet?"

"Ask her what?"

"For cryin' in the rain!"

"Never mind what?!"

"Look Dan, alls I wanna know is, are we goin' swimming tomorrow or not?"

"Oh, ok. I'll ask her."

"When?"

"When what?"

"Jeez Dan, you got potatoes in your ears or

what?...WHEN ARE YOU GOING TO ASK YOUR MOM?...I GOTTA KNOW SO I CAN ASK MINE IF IT'S OK...OK?"

"OK. OK. YOU DON'T HAVE TO YELL! What's with you today anyway?"

"Pass me the green will ya? I need the green."

"Here," I said, handing him the little glass bottle of "Gallant Green."

A few minutes of silence.

"Looks like we're gonna need more blue pretty soon."

"Yeah," he said. "I'll tell my mom to get some on the way to the lake."

"Wait, you mean we're goin'?"

"Well sure. I asked her last night!"

12

In the Kitchen with Dad

As I said, I was only 10 so most of my Saturdays were my own. I loved getting up and going over to Danny's on Saturday just because it was fun; school was over for a few days, and I had an entire weekend ahead of me. Come to think of it, I can't remember feeling any stress at all back then; school was pretty easy, home life was pleasant, and nothing on my ten-year-old body hurt. Of course, this could be selective memory, or just age doing what it'll do sometimes.

So this one Saturday, I woke up earlier than usual. I had a big day ahead of me. I stumbled down the stairs, taking two at a time, just barely missing the post at the end of the

Me and Danny

railing. Still drowsy with sleep, I clumsily made my way to the kitchen. My mom wasn't up yet but my Dad was there, standing in front of the stove with a lit match in his hand.

"This darn stove, we should have gotten rid of it a long time ago," he said to himself.

He bent down and turned the black knob on the front of our huge gas stove, a relic of the postwar era, white enamel, three-feet wide, old-style clock—with hands and a timer—glass windowed oven. He was peering steadily at the front burner, holding his breath…waiting for something to happen.

"C'mon, start" he said through clenched teeth.

All of a sudden, a yellow/blue flame burst out of the front burner. POOF! Dad bolted upright, taking a step backwards at the same time. I could tell that despite nearly getting singed, he was pleased.

"Whoa!" he said. "Almost got me that time. Close, but no cigar, baby."

14

Up until now, he had been so engrossed in his efforts to ignite the burner he hadn't noticed that I was standing behind him.

"Oh! Mike," he said when he turned around, "Didn't see you."

"Morning Dad."

"So, what's got you up so early this morning? Hot date?"

"Very funny Dad. No, just going over to Danny's."

"Then why so early?"

"Danny and I are going to play some golf. He's ahead in the tournament and I just gotta' get even."

"Tournament huh? You mean on that homemade golf course that Dan's brother dug into their backyard? Can't believe his parents let him carve it up like that. All those holes...what are they, sardine cans or something:

"Soup cans. They're soup cans, Dad...oh, and a few tuna fish too."

15

Me and Danny

"Whatever. I hope you don't get any ideas about messing our yard up with that nonsense. At least without telling me about it. Come to think of it, I guess if it's done right…."

"Wow. That would be great. Our very own Par-3 golf course!"

"Hold on now, sport. I didn't say…"

"Yeah, I know I know. I won't hold my breath."

I didn't know it then, but as it turned out, I didn't have to hold my breath very long; by summer's end Dad and I had built our own 9-hole course that stretched from the front yard, through the side yard, and into the backyard! It was even better than the one that Charlie built.

"Did you say something about a tournament? Sounds pretty serious. Did you put a wager on it?"

"Heck yeah. And I'm a little nervous because Dan's been hitting the ball pretty good lately. That, and the fact that there's a king-size Snickers Bar riding on this one!"

"High-stakes game then. So why so early? Gonna get some practice in before the big game?"

"I wish. No, it's his brother Charlie again. We have to play before he gets up so he doesn't get mad. He's such a pain about his precious par 3 course. You'd think it was one of those country clubs you see on television or something. He's worried we'll wreck it, I guess. One time he got so furious with us that he chased us all the way to the school before he gave up! I don't know how you could hurt a bunch of soup cans dug into the ground… but I guess he's just peculiar like that."

"Wow, big word, peculiar. Know what it means?'

"Sure I do. Danny's Dad always uses words like that. It means weird. Kinda like him!"

"Well that's not very nice to say. Mom know where you're going?"

"Sure, it's where I go every Saturday morning."

"All the same, better let her know before you take

17

Me and Danny

off."

"Aw Dad, can't you tell her. I gotta get going."

"O.K., just leave her a note then. You know how she gets when she doesn't know where you kids are."

"I know, but jeez I've been going over to Dan's every Saturday for a hundred years and…."

"Michael…"

"Ok, Ok, I'll leave her a note. Where's some paper?"

"Over there by the phone."

So I scribbled out a note to my Mom, said goodbye to Dad and ran off through the backyard to Danny's.

Charlie Makes an Entrance

When I got over to Danny's house on Clinton Street I was dismayed to see that Charlie was outside in the driveway. I thought that was odd because he hardly ever got up before noon on Saturdays. My heart sank because of what this might mean to our golf game. No way would Charlie let us play now. Anticipating the worst I went around the back to the mud room, a weird little gray room in the back of the house that served as a main entrance and where everybody

Me and Danny

left their boots and coats before going into the kitchen. Danny's house wasn't locked—no one's was back then, so I just turned the white porcelain knob on the back door and let myself in.

Danny was sitting on a low wooden bench just inside the door putting his sneakers on. He looked up and grimaced. I guessed he wasn't happy that his brother was up either.

"What's your brother doing up?"

"Oh, he's helping Mom and Dad."

"Helping them do what?"

"I don't know, something about his friend Darryl."

"Well what about Darryl? Is he in some kind of trouble or something?"

Darryl was Charlie's buddy who, although the same age as Charlie, never seemed to act like it.

"How should I know? Jeez get off my back will ya?"

Danny wasn't such a good sport about his brother.

20

I mean I suppose he loved him and all but he sure didn't seem to like him much. That always surprised me because they were so far apart in age, almost like Charlie was his uncle or something. Not only that, unlike my house, they had separate rooms! They didn't have to sleep in the same room like I had to do with my brother. Heck, they didn't have to sleep in the same *bed* like I did with my brother! And yet they fought just like we did. Go figure.

"Does this mean we can't play golf?" I asked, afraid of the response.

"How should I know?"

"Look do you want me to just go home or what?"

He was being so cranky I thought maybe I'd just as soon take off.

"No, don't go. Sorry, Mike. I'm just frustrated, that's all. It seems that every time we make plans, big fat Charlie has to go and ruin it."

Just then we heard his Mom call from the front of

Me and Danny

the house.

"Charlie, are you ready to go?"

Dan and I jerked our heads toward the voice and held our breath. Did this mean Charlie was leaving? His mom called out again.

"Charlie!"

"Yeah, I'm here! Quit yelling will ya?"

"Well are you ready or not?"

"Yeah I'm ready! Is Dad coming?"

Silence.

"Hey Ma. Is Dad coming?"

A word about Danny's dad; he was older than my dad, a lot older. In fact I remember thinking that he kinda looked and acted like he could have been Dan's grandfather instead of his father. He never spoke...to me anyway. His face was like a muddy road, all rutted up with a huge furrow in his brow. He had eyes that were always sort of half closed, like he was sleepy or something. I guess maybe that was because he was such a voracious reader. He ate books, one after another. I don't know, maybe he was some sort of professor or something; before he got to be an old geezer. Looking back on it, he was probably just a kind, gentle soul who was simply living his life, one day at a time, bringing all he was to all he is.

"Your Dad is on his way out", yelled his mom. "He's just got to put his sweater on."

Dan and I looked up at the same time. Our eyes met; we nodded in triumph. Yes! They were heading out. It looked like we were going to get to play after all. I could taste that Snickers bar already!

Wait....Golf?

As I said, Seneca Falls was a small town back then and there weren't a million ways to have fun, not like there are today. Still, we had a great time playing catch in the street, touch football in the back lot, redlight-green light, hide and seek, and kick the can with the neighbor kids, things like that. Then there were team sports.

Little League baseball was one of the more accessible team sports. But even this sport wasn't a bed of

24

roses for me. Why? Because in those days, baseball fields—at least the kind that kids got to play on— weren't the well-groomed deals they are today. The infield was just coarse gravel, the kind you find at a construction site.

And the ball—that hard, white, stitched-up missile of a thing—kept finding an odd-shaped piece of that gravel, ricocheting unexpectedly, and smacking me in the puss...a lot! Still, I loved playing baseball...that is, until the aforementioned stitched-up missile of thing succeeded in breaking my nose. Yeah, that was it. Time to move on to another sport... I needed to find one that was safer, preferably one in which the ball didn't threaten me.

Enter, golf. Before I met Danny, I knew no one who played the game. Oh, I'd seen it from time to time on the TV when my dad would watch it on Sundays in the dead of winter, more for a psychological lift, evidence that somewhere things were green and sunny, instead of white and desolate, than a passionate interest in the game itself.

25

Me and Danny

Nonetheless, and as unusual as it seems, golf was the new baseball. And Danny and I played it every chance we got.

Now, it seems pretty random, to me at least that golf should have taken on such an important role in my childhood. I mean, the sport wasn't exactly made available to everyone, not like baseball where you needed only a mitt, a ball, and a bat. Golf was a little on the expensive side; between the golf clubs, balls, tees, bags, shoes, and the money you paid to just get onto a golf course, it tended to predict its own clientele so to speak. And my family, as large and loving as it was, didn't have a lot of extra money to spend on anything as frivolous as golf.

Anyhow, Danny and I discovered the game of golf not because we liked the game—we knew nothing about it—but because of his older brother Charlie.

Charlie was quite a bit older than Danny; he was in high school and we were heading into fifth-grade. To me, he seemed a bit of an odd duck, tall and a little clumsy, with a look about him that gave the impression of a person wise beyond his years, like he was born old, if you know what I mean.

He wore his clothes kind of on the loose side which made him look a little tubby, which he really wasn't. Sometimes he acted, well, just like an older brother; a little annoyed that he had a little brother at all. But that said, he was a pretty decent guy. And, he was on the high school golf team which meant that he had lots of golf equipment lying around: clubs, balls, tees, bags, towels, head covers, cleats, stuff like that. So naturally Danny and I—being the resourceful ten-year-olds that we were—thought it only fitting that we should borrow Charlie's equipment whenever the mood struck us.

Most of the time Charlie didn't mind us using these extra things he had. But when he did mind…he *really* minded, carrying on about Dan not taking care of his stuff and how when Charlie let us use his stuff Dan didn't appreciate it and maybe he wouldn't let us use anything anymore.

I remember this one time:

We were in the side yard on the 6th hole of Charlie's makeshift golf course. Dan had just chipped his first shot when he heard an angry voice coming from the back of the house.

"Dan! Where are you?" Charlie shrieked.

Despite his age, he was in high school at the time, Charlie's voice sometimes cracked like a kid's. He was way past puberty so it always surprised me how suddenly his voice would break into that creaky falsetto.

"Dan! Where the heck are you?" he shrieked.

Dan and I stiffened like a couple of soldiers being called to attention. We didn't get to answer. Before we knew it, here comes Charlie stomping around the lilac bush like his horse was in the ditch and his hair on fire. Funny, but at the time I remember thinking how if this were a cartoon, he

28

would've had eyes bugging out of his head and steam shooting from his ears.

We looked at each other with that 'jeez-what-did-we-do-this-time' look. We heard the crackle of breaking branches. Then, there he was: big as life and twice as real.

"How many times do I have to tell you", he spit.

"Clean off my irons after you mess 'em up? I pulled my three iron out in the match today and I could hardly tell it was an iron, there was so much mud on it!"

"Why you yellin' at me? It's *your* club, not mine."

"Yeah but you used it didn't you?"

"What are you talking about? When?"

"Yesterday," he spat.

"I wasn't even home yesterday you idiot!"

"What are you talking about, yes you were. You and Mike took 'em over to the field didn't you?"

"We didn't go to the field yesterday!"

Now it was Dan who was mad. Charlie was always

29

getting things confused and whenever he did, he would blame Dan.

"Oh, that's right," Charlie said pensively.

"Yeah, that's right Charlie! You took them to practice yesterday, remember?"

"Oh, well never mind then," Charlie said over his shoulder as he skulked back to the house.

"Yeah, never mind."

"Idiot!" Dan yelled…after his brother was a safe distance away.

Yep...Golf!

Despite the occasional blow-ups, I gotta say we never had any major problems with Charlie, not really. And to tell you the truth, without Charlie, Danny and I would have never learned to play golf. Not only did he loan us his clubs, he also built one heckuva miniature golf course on the property that surrounded their house.

Charlie's 'golf course' was a nine-hole "pitch and putt" kind of deal. Here in the Northeast, we call them Par 3 courses, on account of you're supposed to make it to the hole in three shots or less.

The holes on his homemade course were empty soup and tuna fish cans sunk into the ground, flush with the grass. The course was spread out among the trees, bushes, and the one garden shed his father built. Starting in the backyard ten feet from the mudroom steps, it had nine holes, each one of them different in terms of normal backyard hazards: mud puddles, thorn bushes, low-hanging tree limbs. For example, the first hole was one of the longest on the course but not very tough, not like the 7th. The 7th was short but had some serious hazards: high pricker bushes on both sides, a shallow depression that was always wet. Stuff like that.

The idea of our game was to start at the first hole and basically see how many strokes it took to hit the ball into the hole. The one with the fewest strokes—shots—at the end of nine holes won. What made it really cool was that it was real golf. Thanks to Charlie we got to use real golf clubs, not some homemade deals we'd slapped together in the shed. We actually got to play golf the way real golfers play on real golf courses. Also, it was right there in the lawn around the house which meant we could play almost anytime we wanted to. And just like real golf, there were some pretty demanding skills involved. It was both cool and challenging at the same time, in other words, fun.

For example, because the course had just nine short holes, just one bad shot could cost us the match. Every shot counted. We couldn't afford to make any big mistakes; if our concentration lapsed during a swing, even for a moment, it could cost us big-time. And when the stakes were as high as a ten-cent Snickers bar, well...

Eye-hand coordination was key as well. To make a decent shot, the club had to strike the ball at precisely the right time and at the right angle. If the clubface hit the ball at the wrong angle, the direction the ball traveled could end up

33

being way off. A player's swing was vital to the outcome of the match from the very start.

The first shot, called the tee shot, is very important because it can sometimes determine the outcome of the hole. If the shot goes too far, chances are very good that the ball will be unplayable on account of the fact that the course is really just someone's backyard. It could land in a ditch or end up lodged in a bush or something. Either way, you're really hard-pressed to come up with a good follow-up shot.

But despite the skill aspect of the game, sometimes a good shot on Charlie's course could be just plain old dumb luck. This was because unlike a professional golf course which is well-groomed and manicured, our Par 3 course was rough and ungroomed. It had all the imperfections you'd expect to find in anyone's backyard: sticks, stones, bushes, trees, dandelions, ruts, little toy cars, toads, moles and who knows what else. So in addition to skill, it also helped when just by luck, you got a good bounce after hitting one of these.

34

Nothing pleased us more than seeing a badly hit ball land smack dab on some random tree branch, then watching it ricochet off toward the hole! Boy, that kind of dumb luck would make us howl every time, no matter whose shot it was!

In addition to all of this, there was the weather. Sometimes rain, sometimes snow, yes, we played in the snow, sometimes wind. If it was raining, the course got so muddy; we ended up spending more time wiping our clubs off than actually swinging them. If it was snowing, it was hard to find the ball... even if it landed right in front of us—white on white you know. And wind was just a wild card, sometimes working in our favor, sometimes not.

Well, when the Snickers bar match finally arrived, the day dawned without a cloud in the sky: no rain, no wind. It was a real humdinger, let me tell you. And in addition to good weather, we also had a course that was in as good shape as it ever was on account of Charlie having mowed the day before. The conditions were perfect for the big game.

Me and Danny

Taking up our positions on the first tee, we shot fingers to see who was going to get to hit first. One-two-three shoot! Danny won with four fingers to my two. He lined up his shot, took a swing, and smacked it. It was a good one, landing just three feet from the hole. I was up against it right off the bat.

I took my stance with the ball a little to the right of center, just the way I like it. After taking a deep breath, I began my back swing. As my club was heading down toward the ball, a car went by.

"HONK, HONK,... HONK HONK"

Now it just so happened that the first tee was right next to the sidewalk that ran along Mynderse Street so when the horn went off, it was as if we were standing right next to it. Of course I hadn't seen the car coming so the sound scared the heck out of me. I must have jerked my arms when the horn started blaring because when the club hit the ball, instead of going straight toward the hole, the ball sailed right over the hedge and into the neighbor's yard!

I looked up quickly. I wanted to see who was driving this car that caused me to blow my shot. I must have had a comical look on my face because no sooner that I raised my head than Danny burst out laughing. He could hardly talk he was laughing so hysterically.

"Oh man, ha ha ha! Now THERE'S one for the books! Real Pretty! Ha ha ha!"

"Oh nice Dan! Thanks a lot," I sputtered.

"I blow just one shot and you laugh! Thanks a lot pal. I'll remember that."

"No, no." he said. "It was just that you looked so mad! Your face was all contorted. It was like you had steam blowing out your ears like Bugs Bunny or something."

He continued to laugh at me until I asked him who it was that made me miss the shot. He stopped laughing and said,

"Oh that was Darryl, Charlie's buddy. He always

37

blows his horn when he passes the house. You know, just in case Charlie's home. My Dad hates it."

"Gosh, it seems even when Charlie's not home, he causes some sort of trouble for us," I complained.

"Ha ha, yeah, I guess you're right. Let's play. You can take that one over if you want to."

"Really? Neat. Thanks."

"But if I were you, I think I'd wait 'till there's no cars going by!" Dan said.

Dan went on to win that first hole—even after I got to take that horrible first shot over. The next hole was a short one; it began just to the right of a big pricker bush and headed straight for an old apple tree by the basketball hoop.

"All right, you're up." I said to Dan as we walked to the starting point. "Don't get cocky, now. The day's young."

Dan picked up his 9-iron and swung a few times for practice. He looked hard toward the hole. We never *really* knew exactly where the holes were located, kinda tough sticking flags into rusty old soup cans.

He took a few more practice strokes.

"Uh, you gonna hit the ball at some point?"

"Keep your shirt on, will ya?"

"It's on, already. So is this tournament."

"All right, all right. Here goes…"

Dan swung his 9-iron. But instead of hitting the ball, it scrubbed the grass just in front of it. This sent the ball scudding along the ground, stopping not more than five feet in front of us.

"Ugh!" Dan grunted. "Man…that's what I get for hurrying."

"You want a Mulligan on that one?" I asked, meaning do you want to take another shot without being penalized?

"Is that OK?" he asked.

"Sure, I suppose so. We just started and we're sorta getting warmed up."

Me and Danny

"Thanks." Dan said.

"But whaddya say we don't allow Mulligans from now on. Just so we can like, finish this game before we're both in wheelchairs."

Dan chuckled.

"You got it."

Dan went on to win that hole as well. He had a five. I flubbed my first shot…again…and it took me 6 strokes to make into the hole.

The following hole was a much longer one, extending from that old apple tree near the basketball hoop all the way to the tree house.

Dan's first shot was a good one but his next one landed in the lilac trees near the driveway. My first shot was a doozy, landing just a few feet from the hole.

"Man, that was a great shot!" Dan said. "Kind of like you had that one on a string and the hole just pulled it ahead."

"Thanks." Pure skill is what that was." I said, sticking out my ten-year-old chest.

"Yeah, that was skill all right. Luck had nothing to do with that shot. Right…for sure. Like my old granny it didn't!" he shot back.

The rest of the game went on like this; Dan winning some holes, me winning some. When we reached the final hole—the longest one that stretched along the back side of the house, bending around a big oak tree then bee-lining it toward the hole next to the neighbor's driveway, we were even-steven at 48 strokes apiece.

"All right, this is it, Dan." I said, reaching for a 7-iron.

"Yep." he said. "Prepare to be beaten."

"Prepare to fork over that King-Size Snickers, fella." I said.

I took a few practice strokes. Then a few more.

"While we're still young, Mike. While we're still

41

young." Dan said, trying to hurry me up.

"All right, all right. Settle down." I said.

I swung the club. The ball bounced straight up and landed not more than ten feet in front of us.

"Aw. That's too bad, Mike. Really. Couldn't have happened to a nicer kid."

"Never mind the jokes, Dan. You're up. Let's see how you make out."

Dan took his 8-iron and swung it a few times.

"You sure about that? An 8?" Might be longer than it looks you know. And the ground…it's a little…"

Dan cut me off.

"Hey, did I bug you when it was your turn?"

"All right. I'll shut up." I said.

"Well, that would be just ducky. Thanks loads." he said.

Dan swung his club and hit the ball perfectly. His shot was beautiful, a nice high arch, straight and true. It

42

landed in a perfect placement for his next shot. Mine, meanwhile, landed in the high grass near a big bush and was tucked delicately right under a nice big dandelion weed, hardly visible.

We grabbed our clubs and walked toward my ball. As my shot landed farthest from the hole, it was my turn to hit.

"All right. Watch this, Dan." I said confidently, eyeing the thorns surrounding the weed.

"I'm watching. I feel for you, bub. Can you even see what you're aiming at? Pretty deep grass here in the rough. Charlie was supposed to weed the lawn when he mowed. Guess he forgot." Dan said.

For a minute it occurred to me that Dan had planned this and that it may have been his turn to mow, and he didn't weed on account of it giving him an advantage.

"You say it was Charlie's turn to mow and weed the lawn?"

Me and Danny

"Yeah." he said.

"You sure? You didn't plan this did you? I mean not weeding the lawn so you could maybe have a home field advantage or something?"

"What? How in the world would that've helped? I mean think about it…we're playing the same course at the same time! You think I have a personal relationship with every blade of grass or something?" Dan asked.

This made me think.

"Oh, yeah. Right. I guess that would make no sense."

"Yeah. Hey, I tell you what? Why don't you just swing the club and let's get on with this. I'm hungry."

"Oh. So you can taste that Snickers bar already can you? You think you're gonna take this tournament? Do you?" I asked, smiling.

"Just hit the ball, for the love of Pete."

I swung. It sounded good. I didn't look up, afraid of

where the ball would land after being so tucked into the weeds as it was.

"Whoa!" Dan yelled.

I looked up. And what do you know? The ball disappeared.

"Wait." I said. "What happened? Where's the ball? Where'd it go? Dan. Did you see it?"

We silently walked toward the neighbor's driveway to the last hole.

"Dan, what the heck happened to my ball? Did you see it or what?"

Dan said nothing.

We finally reached the hole and peered into it together. There it was, snuggled right in the bottom of the Campbell's soup can!

"Well, I'll be," I said.

"Well, I'll be," Dan said.

"You are a lucky skunk," he said.

45

Me and Danny

"A lucky HUNGRY skunk," I shot back.

And with that, we put our clubs back in the shed and headed toward Tizivani's corner store and my king-size Snickers!

Down a Lonely Dirt Road

Before I leave the subject of golf and the hours of enjoyment Dan and I got from screwing around with it, there was another activity that was just as much fun as backyard golf, and perhaps a little less risky in terms of arousing the Wrath of Charlie.

A little background...in the game of golf, the first shot is known as a drive. This is where the golfer balances his ball on top of a golf tee, steps back and wails at it as hard as he can. The trick is to hit it as far as possible in as straight a line as you can.

Seeing as how the Wiggins's yard wasn't big enough—that is without one of us 'expert' golfers shanking a ball right through one of the neighbors' window— we had to find another place to practice our drives. It didn't take us long to come up with the perfect place. Our old school, Frank M. Knight Elementary, was just down the street a few blocks. The playground was surrounded by a huge field that put plenty of space between our golf balls and the school's windows. We often went there to horse around: hit golf balls, play football, climb trees in the woods around the field, act a fool on the playground and collect insects for our insect collections, the ones we kept in old cigar boxes.

Now about the golf ball situation…after a few practice sessions over at Frank Knight—spraying them all over the place, losing lots of them in the tall weeds bordering the field— it became obvious that we'd have to have lots and lots of them if we were going to continue playing. At first, we 'borrowed' a few from Charlie's stash. But after catching us palming a few from his golf bag—and going a little nuts yelling at us, threatening to take away access to his beloved backyard golf course–Charlie came up with a plan; he started counting all his golf balls, even the sliced up ones! Danny and I were cut off. It was a lesson well-learned: don't be messing with Charlie's golf balls, not if you want to keep playing tournaments on his homemade course.

We needed golf balls; this was clear. But we no longer had access to Charlie's stash and we certainly couldn't buy them—we were only 10 and had no money to speak of—so we had to find a place where we could 'find' them. Where? Well, where else? Where actual golfers play golf, on an actual golf course. It was easy to figure out which one, on account of back then, we only had one: The Seneca Falls Country Club. It was a cinch that we weren't the only ones

Me and Danny

who couldn't hit balls in a straight line, so by golly, that's where we should go.

Now to help us figure out just how this would work, we took a chance; we asked the only real golfer we knew: Charlie. Naturally neither Danny nor I thought that he'd lift a finger to help us; after all, he'd just forbidden us from using any of his, then threatened to take away our golfing privileges on his course. But lo and behold, he did…help us that is. He told us about this one hole, one of the hardest holes on the course, that happened to have a road running right alongside it the whole way. We figured that in the woods between this road and the fairway, the woods being where the balls are *not* supposed to go and the fairways being where the balls *are* supposed to go, we'd find the ones that the golfers hooked into the woods and couldn't find.

The problem was this: The Country Club was quite a way's away from Dan's house. This meant that Danny would have to ask, annoy, and otherwise pester his mom to take us. It was one thing to plead with her to give us a ride down the lake to take a dip on a sweltering summer day; it was another to ask her to take time out of her day so we could go on...of all things, a golf ball hunt, never mind that it was probably trespassing to boot!

The more we thought about it, the less likely it seemed. For starters, it was a good six or seven miles away. This wasn't great but what made it even worse was the fact that this road that Charlie told us about wasn't paved; it was dirt! And being dirt meant that her black car would come back to the house, brown. More reason to say no, we thought.

On the other hand, we really needed some balls you know, so we could practice our drives. Why the big rush? Simple. It was summer, school was out, we were 10, and this is what we wanted to do.

So, one bright, beautiful summer day we decided to risk it. We decided to approach Danny's mom about driving us way out of town. To find a long, dusty dirt road that we'd never been on—and weren't really sure existed in the first place—to trespass on private property. Then turn around and come back to pick us up somewhere along the same stretch of dirt road, just so we could beat the bushes for little white balls.

"You sure you wanna do this?" I asked.

"No…not really," Danny said.

"Well, we need some balls, Dan. How many do you have right now?"

Danny shoved his hands into the pockets of his jeans, dug around a little.

"Three. No wait…" he said, walking over to the shed where Charlie kept his golfing gear. While he was in there, I dug around in my pockets to see how many I had. A few minutes later Dan came out. He wasn't smiling.

"Shoot, Mike. I thought I had a few squirreled away in there, but naw, I couldn't find 'em. Charlie evidently did though, the big lug. How many do you have?"

"Same...three I guess."

"Well," Dan said with resignation in his voice. "I guess we need to decide if we really want more."

"What?" I blurted. "Whaddya mean 'if we really want more.' Of course we do. With only six balls between us, we'll be lucky to play at all. Not the way you've been hitting them lately."

Danny's head shot up.

"Me?" he squeaked. "The way *I've* been hitting them? Whaddya talking about? Who shanked three of them into the pond the other day? The way *I've* been hittin' them...Ha!"

"All right, all right. But that doesn't change things. We really need to decide...and today. We've got all weekend to play..."

"OK. I say we go for it," Dan said with even more resignation in his voice.

Me and Danny

"Yeah, m too. Let's go for it," I said. "Let's go right in there and ask your mom to take us out there, to that road that Charlie told us about this morning."

So it was decided. We were going to ask Dan's mom if she wouldn't mind driving us out to where Charlie said there was a road that ran parallel to some hole on the Seneca Falls Golf Course…some road way out of town that maybe existed, maybe we could find, and maybe would yield the golf balls we really, really needed.

"We" did the deciding. "We" didn't go in together.

I waited outside…Danny went into the house to ask. He was in there a long time, long enough for me to play an entire game of P.I.G. by myself on the basketball court outside the back door. I didn't hear any yelling so I was hopeful. And you know what? The next thing I know here comes Danny banging out the back door with this huge grin on his face!

"Looks like we're goin'!" he yells as he trips down

the stairs.

"Really?" I yelled. What'd she say? Is she really gonna to take us? When? How'd you do it?"

"She just said 'OK' and that was about it. I told her what Charlie told us and she said she'd talk to him about where to go and then she just said 'OK.'"

Sometimes adults can surprise you.

Not ten minutes later we're in the car. Dan's mom is driving and she's following our directions toward the road that we'd heard about, the one running alongside the 2nd fairway. We're both in the back seat like we're in a taxi or something, giving directions as if we'd been driving for years and actually knew what we were doing. She was telling us—convincing herself more like it—that she could remember where it was that Charlie told her to go.

It went on like this for about ten minutes until we came to a clearing in the woods along the road. We peered through the trees and saw golfers walking along the fairway

Me and Danny

on the golf course. We'd found it!

"Wait. Slow down. I think we found it," Dan yelled.

His mom jammed on the brakes. Before the car came to a full stop Danny and I were already halfway out the door, running for the woods.

Looking back on it, I'm not entirely sure it was quite a safe thing to do; dropping off two ten-year-olds on the side of a lonely dirt road in the middle of nowhere to go off trespassing on the grounds of a private golf club. But we went, and not just once. I guess it just goes to show you; sometimes things can simply work out, even if the odds are against it.

The times that we could convince his mom to cart us out there, it was always the same procedure. Danny and I would just skulk around in the woods carrying our plastic grocery store sacks trying to avoid the gaze of any golfers who happened to be playing the hole, dodging the poison ivy and poison oak, all the time searching for little dots of white among the green, brown, and gray of the woods.

Every time we found a ball hidden in that mosquito-infested woods, we'd give out a little yelp! Both to punctuate that thrill as well as to make sure another ball was added to our count; everything was a competition back then, a friendly, good-natured one. I can almost feel it now, some 60 years later.

Sometimes we came home with dozens of them: some all sliced up, some brand new. And some no doubt very sorely missed; shiny right-out-of-the-package signature golf balls, the kind that golfers hate to lose.

In addition to searching for golf balls in the woods next to the 2nd hole fairway, these trips provided great entertainment in the form of human adult behavior. We saw some great temper tantrums I tell you; grown men swearing and carrying on like ill-mannered two-year-olds, reduced to childish fits of rage. Personally I found it both enlightening as well as entertaining to see some so-called "pillar of the community" having a complete nervous breakdown over losing a golf ball or flubbing a shot. Owners of prominent Fall Street businesses, councilmen, little league baseball coaches, red-faced and bellowing like sick cows, pitching clubs into water hazards, tossing putters into the woods ...it was great fun for me—at 10—to see guys decades older—and presumably more mature—acting my age instead of theirs...boy, you couldn't *pay* to see a show like that!

The Tree Fort

One of the most exciting things Danny and I ever did together was to build our tree fort. We were at the age when boys just have to build a tree fort. It's just something that you have to do, like a biological necessity. If you opened up any ten-year-old boy on the planet, you'd find a gene that looked something like a miniature fort. We were no exception.

Me and Danny

We built this fort all by ourselves in a grand old apple tree in Danny's backyard, on the property line as far away from his house as one could get without trespassing onto the neighbor's yard. Mind you, neither one of us really knew one end of a hammer from the other. That didn't faze us in the least. We were going to build a tree fort, no matter what...plain and simple.

So every day after school, Danny and I would take a beat-up Radio Flyer red wagon and go on long searches for scraps of building materials. Being a small town, word got out quickly. It seemed that the whole town was helping us. Neighbors, grocery store clerks, lumberyard guys all knew us by name. They'd let us know whenever they had a used kitchen door, a spare stick of lumber, a bag of rusty nails, stuff like that.

The old apple tree itself was tailor-made for a fort. Its branches, gnarled and craggy as they were, provided a nice little nesting area right in the middle. It was just begging for

60

an odd little home away from home. And, it was an apple tree, which meant that it gave us an unlimited amount of apples—the ripe ones we ate, the ones with worms…we chucked!

I had helped my Dad around the house more than Danny had—on account of his Dad being, like I said, old and all, so I got to be the foreman. Yeah, I got the final say whenever an argument came up. Questions of bracing, nail size, branch selection.

We hardly ever used a saw—maybe we didn't have one, maybe our ten-year-old skills weren't up to the task, I don't remember. In any event, it meant that Danny and I had to use all the stuff people gave us the way they gave it. (As my dear mother would always say: 'beggars can't be choosers.') If Mr. Lapinsky gave us a splintery 10-foot plank, we'd find a place for it as it was. Mr. Jenkins' kitchen door remained a kitchen door, except now it was a floor. Mrs. Dellafave's garage door panel stayed a garage door panel until

Me and Danny

it was nailed up as a wall.

Our fort didn't happen overnight. Working after school till dinner time and Saturdays after cartoons, it was weeks until it was finished. But boy, it was a pretty snazzy place, I must say. Three floors, a trap door, a foolproof enemy resistant front entrance, three windows and a sun deck…awesome! Of course the floors weren't level, the walls leaned in and out, and the makeshift roof kept the snow out but not the rain. Yet, warts and all, it was all ours. Danny and I built the Mother of all tree forts; it was our fortress.

Before climbing up into the fort, we'd first stop down at our corner candy store, Tizivani's Red and White. Tizivani's was just a block away from Danny's place on the corner of Daniels and Mynderse Streets. It was one of those neighborhood stores that were so prevalent back in the day. Every neighborhood had one. Sometimes they were just someone's front porch that they loaded up with boxes of penny candy, the kind that kids could afford. Sometimes they

Michael Cerza

were actual grocery stores stocked with staples such as bread, milk, eggs, flour, and sugar, the stuff that your mom could ask you to jump on your bike and get.

Now penny candy, what a thing that was. Candy that cost a penny. Imagine. I could go in with a nickel, which equaled a deposit from a single empty coke bottle I found on the street somewhere, and come out with a pocketful of fireballs, caramels, MaryJanes, taffy, Boston Baked Beans or a million other confections. Back then candy bars cost a dime...and not the little ones but the king-size bars! Fireballs two for a penny, ten-cent candy bars and nickel cokes. Life was good.

Anyway, that neighborhood store of ours, what a great place to go. The building itself stands out in my memory. It was brick. And on long summer days when daylight edged closer to dusk and it was getting on time to go home, I remember the way the side of the building used to turn brownish orange. Funny, of all the things that happen in

63

Me and Danny

a lifetime, the things that linger in memory…

One more thing: the Tizivanis. As a youngster growing up in a rather homogenous village in Upstate New York, I never gave a thought to their heritage; they were just the folks who owned the neighborhood IGA store on the corner. I kind of wish it was like that nowadays; people just being people, no preconceived notions about anything, just plain folks. Simplistic? Maybe. Needed? Absolutely.

Anyway, the Tizivanis lived over their corner IGA store, in an apartment that spanned the whole top floor. They had a daughter my age. The curious thing is that I never saw her. I don't know why, but I never saw her. I didn't even know her name, still don't. I remember her dad though, a tall, barrel-chested, dark-haired guy, not particularly friendly. Whenever Danny and I came into the store he'd watch us, you know, just to make sure we didn't steal anything, especially in the candy aisle. He wasn't mean or anything, but he wasn't nice either. I guess he was only watching out for himself but he didn't need to; we never stole anything.

Once Danny and I had paid a visit to the store and gotten ourselves some candy, we'd go back to our fort. What a wonderful feeling it was to climb up through the trap door, past the first platform and on up to the roof of our very own little fortress from which we could look out upon our kingdom, squinting beneath the brims of our baseball caps, arms bent to our hips in classic Superman pose, feeling the clean breezes of summer. There we'd remain, silent except for the munching of candy bars, the slurping of glass-bottled cokes and the rustling of comic book pages.

Speaking of comic books, Danny and I saw eye to eye on lots of stuff. But we parted company when it came to our choice of comic book superheroes.

My favorite comic was The Fantastic Four. Like all of us back then, superhero and citizen alike, the Fantastic Four's main job was defending truth, justice, and the American way. Having gained their superpowers because of

Me and Danny

an over-exposure to cosmic rays during a scientific space voyage, they each had different powers. Three of them were family members. Ben was just a friend: a grumpy, heart-of-gold gentle-giant type friend. He was my favorite. Don't get me wrong; the others could do some cool stuff too: turn themselves into fire, stretch into any shape or size, be invisible. But I really liked Ben's sentimental approach to eliminating evil. Whenever he had to crush or stomp an evildoer, he did it with a kindness that bordered on compassion.

Dan liked Superman. He could fly and he could make diamonds out of lumps of coal and whatnot. But as I tried to tell him a thousand times—he was only one guy, whereas the Fantastic Four were…well…four. They could beat Superman up with one hand tied behind their backs. Despite our differences, Danny and I never took this comic book rivalry very seriously. We were best friends and we were having the time of our young lives.

Michael Cerza

You Wanna What?

One Saturday afternoon in the summer of 1962, Danny and I decided to go over to Frank Knight and practice our tee shots. We loved doing this; it felt so good to have all the time in the world to just smack some balls around, to feel like there was nothing better to do, to get better at it, then feel good about that too. Naturally we needed lots of

Me and Danny

practice, seeing as how we were only 10. So we grabbed a couple of old drivers out of the tool shed, thank you Charlie, and took off for the neighborhood fairway.

Danny and I began driving balls, teeing them up at one end of the field and hitting them until we reached the other end. Years later when I actually started playing golf for real, the time I spent smacking those balls around gave me a leg-up on this crazy and decidedly improbable game. For Danny and me though, it was just some good, clean, fifth-grade fun.

We had only been hitting about a half hour when Danny stopped me in mid-stroke.

"Hey!!" he yelled as my club was just starting its downward stroke.

"What the..." I said, trying futilely to stop the motion of the club.

It was too late; I flubbed it bad; the face of my driver slammed into the muddy grass just behind the ball, a classic 'dub.'

THUD!

Danny and I watched the ball skitter a few feet in front of us then skitter to a stop. The wooden tee lay splintered at our feet.

"What are you trying to do anyway? That was going to be a great shot! Jeez, Dan."

"Hey look. Over there." He said as he pointed with the head of his 3 wood.

"Where?"

"Over there where I'm pointing."

"Yeah, so…what do you want me to…." I began, stopping short to have a look. Then I saw it: a break in the long line of reflecting glass windows.

"Look. It's open."

"Yeah, I see it. Big deal, an open window. Something new for you, Dan?"

"No. Shut up. I have an idea. Let's go in. This is

our big chance, Mike. What do you say? Let's bust into the school."

"What? Are you crazy? What if someone's in there? We'd get caught."

"Nobody's there. It's Saturday."

"Yeah, that's true. And it sure looks empty. It's all dark inside."

"Well, what do you say? Want to?"

"You?"

"Sure, why not?"

"Well ok, but let's be careful ok? I don't want to get into any trouble."

"Oh stop being a big baby. C'mon. Let's go."

The window that Dan was pointing to was open it's true, but it wasn't going to be a cinch to climb through it. This type of window was typical of the windows they used to put in schools back then. Hinged at the top, they swing open like an awning over a storefront display window. They didn't open all the way like a regular double-hung window, the kind in your house. It'd be one heckuva challenge to scramble through this one for sure. If we did decide to go through with this, we'd have to wriggle our way up and over the metal ridge of the window and get through the small opening. I guess they put these windows in schools for a reason.

Of course, we had no intention of causing any harm if by some fluke we did make it inside, none whatsoever. We didn't want to mess anything up or anything, we simply wanted to go in and have a look around, for old time's sake. We 'graduated' from elementary school the year before and had moved on to junior high; this was just, I don't know, maybe something we thought big kids did.

Danny and I, having decided to at least pursue the idea a little more, started to tap our balls in the direction of the open window, casual like, just in case anyone happened to be watching. As we nonchalantly walked toward the school, my mind traveled back to the times when we actually

Me and Danny

went to school there.

It was only a few years ago in terms of real, adult-time years, but from the perspective of a ten-year-old, it seemed like ages since we walked those long halls, ate in that low-ceilinged cafeteria and played dodgeball in that cavernous elementary gymnasium.

I could see the teachers, the hallways, the gym, the cloak room, and my kindergarten classroom. I flashed on the time MaryJane Smith grabbed me by my five-year-old shoulders and punched my cheek with her pursed lips while we were sitting inside that cool, cardboard igloo...my first kiss. I could hear the glass milk bottles and the rattling sound they made in their little loose-wheeled trolley as I pushed it down the hall to each classroom, see the erasers I got to clap clean on the side of the brick school building for doing as I was told, feel the spanking in 2nd-grade for not.

Tap, tap, tap, closer and closer to the school we got with each poke until suddenly we found ourselves standing right in front of the open window. I looked at our old school; it seemed smaller to me somehow. Maybe I was feeling bigger.

Danny and I turned away from the school and scanned the area, left to right, right to left as far we could see. We looked back at each other. Our eyes met and we each gave a silent nod as if to say, "*ok, this is it…you really want to do this? There's no turning back once we touch this building.*"

Then without a word Danny dropped his clubs and jumped up onto the sill of the open window. He balanced himself there for a moment, changed his grip on the top of the window frame then jammed his upper torso into the opening. We were making this up as we went along, so we had no idea if it was even possible, heck for all we knew we'd end up getting stuck then having to run for help! This could be bad.

Danny paused for a moment, then with one last push, he scrambled up and into the open window, smashing

Me and Danny

his knees, ankles, and head on the metal framework.

"Ugh!"

He managed to change his grip again, and pulling with all his might, squeezed through the opening and onto the floor inside, taking what sounded like a whole library of books with him.

Fa...flut...ump...crash!

Holy cow, I thought. *We're really doing this! There's really no turning back now! I have to do what Danny just did; we're breaking into our old school!*

With my heart pounding, and my mind reeling, I jumped up onto the sill like Danny did, grabbed whatever I could and wedged my body into the window opening. That's when I heard a loud RIP! My T-shirt had gotten snagged on one of the metal pieces of the window frame.

"Dan! Dan!, I hissed in a loud whisper. I'm caught. I can't move!"

"Jeez," he whispered. Keep quiet, willya? You

74

wanna get us caught? Wait. I see the problem. Hold on, just stay still."

"Yeah, ok. Like that's easy. I'm caught! Do something!"

"Keep your shirt on will ya? I gotta think."

A thought streaks across my mind: *Keep your shirt on…that's funny—or at least it would be if I wasn't in this mess…what the heck am I doin' breaking into a public building—I don't want a criminal record for cryin' out loud!*

OK, this is Awesome!

From inside the school, Danny reached up through the open window. But the angle was so severe he couldn't find where my shirt was caught. I was halfway in and halfway out; I suddenly realized that anyone who happened to be passing by would be able to see me.

"Dan! Dan! What do we do? I can't move. I'm

stuck!

I realized that my voice was much louder than it should have been but a moment of terror seized me; I couldn't help it.

"Stay still will ya? I'm working on it"

"C'mon hurry up. They can see me!"

"Who? Who can see you? Is someone out there? Jeez, Mike is someone out there?"

"I don't know. I can't see. I can't move to look around behind me. Hurry up, hurry up!"

RIP!!

All at once, I felt my shirt give way accompanied by a sharp stab in my shoulder.

"Ow! Ow!" I screamed.

For a split second I wanted to cut and run. But then I realized Danny was pulling me, dragging me, through the window!

"AH! UGH!" I grunted. The next thing I knew I

Me and Danny

felt something sharp poking my knee and my arm at the same time. Then, boom! My body fell like a sack of potatoes—dumping me inside the school and onto something soft. I was in!

As I lay there on the cold classroom floor, my legs entangled with Dan's, I tried to make sense of where we landed. The classroom was dark. Our eyes were used to the sunlit playground; we were blind. Grunting and groaning, we untied our limbs.

"Hey get offa me will ya'?" said Dan.

"Waddya think I'm tryin to do…jeez.," I said.

"Well try harder will ya'? Wait…that's my foot…watch out for my foot!"

"Hey, not so loud," I whispered.

"Waddya' tryin' to do, get us caught or something?"

"I can't see anything! Where are we for cryin' out loud?"

"How should I know? Here, move your leg a little,

we almost got it."

"There. You alright?"

"Yeah, you?"

"Yeah."

Our hearts were pounding out of our little chests. We scrambled to our feet and began to survey our new environment. We looked to the front of the classroom. The green chalkboard was wiped clean, the chairs upside down on top of the desks, legs sticking straight up into the mysterious darkness.   As we swung our eyes toward the back of the room, they caught on a bright light shining across the forest of chairs.

"Hey, you see that?" I said, whispering again.

"What the heck is it?"

"Man, I don't know. Maybe this wasn't such a good idea."

"Hold on. I can almost see." Dan said, rubbing his eyes.

Me and Danny

Neither Danny nor I seemed to be able to move. Our P.F Flyers stuck fast to the cold floor right inside the windows through which we had just tumbled.

"Dan?"

"What."

"Maybe we should just get outta here, huh?" I said, still trying to adjust to the darkness.

I peered through the skinny window of the classroom door. It was incredibly bright...like the midafternoon-day's sun was right outside the door. It played in stark contrast with the blackness of the classroom—so much so that it sparked a momentary flashback of Danny and I sitting side by side in the cool dark of the Strand Theater the week before, munching on candy bars, waiting to see a Superman cartoon. The thought comforted me.

Suddenly, Danny's voice snapped me back to reality.

"Naw, c'mon let's take a look out there," he said, and began walking toward the door.

With our eyes opened as wide as possible, we picked our way gingerly through the desks and chairs of the dark classroom. We were careful not to snag our t-shirts on a chair leg, remembering what a racket they made when they fell off the desks.

As we edged closer to the door, the bright light pouring from the classroom door's window blinded us momentarily.

"Jeez, that's bright." Dan said between clenched teeth.

"Yeah. Hey look out for that wastebasket!" I half-yelled.

It was too late. Dan's foot caught it broadside and sent it scudding loudly across the polished floor. It stopped when it hit a metal supply cabinet.

CRASH! SHHISHH... BLAM!

We held our breath. If someone was in the school, they sure as heck heard that!

81

Me and Danny

Silence.

We stood stock still like a couple of cigar store Indians, our ears straining, listening for a reason to high-tail it back outside.

Suddenly I felt hot all over. The thought of trying to stuff myself back through that window was not very appealing. It was tough enough getting in. What if I couldn't do it? I began to sweat.

"Nice goin'!" I hissed.

"Hey, it wasn't my fault. I can't see anything!"

"Yeah? Well neither can I. But you don't see ME running into things!"

For a moment, neither of us said anything. My mind was a ball of confusion.

We just broke into the school!

Wow, this is really neat!

What the heck are we doing? We're criminals for cryin' out loud.

Let's keep going!

More thoughts:

Holy Toledo! What if someone finds us? My parents are gonna kill me! I wonder what the principal's office looks like when nobody's there!'

I don't know how long we stood there, silent, motionless, alone with our own thoughts, listening to each other's' breathing…it seemed an eternity.

"I think it's ok," whispered Dan.

"Yeah me too," I whispered back.

The light shone with increasing brightness as we approached the door. In my mind I knew that many familiar sights were on the other side; it was comforting and worrisome at the same time. Danny was in front of me. He reached for the knob. I looked over his shoulder into the bright hallway and recognized the yellow wall tiles of the hallway.

Then a strange thing happened. Somewhere in my

Me and Danny

mind, something shifted and I slipped into a memory.

I was in Mrs. Martin's 3rd-grade class. It was just before morning recess. We had just finished a writing exercise when an alarm sounded. We were accustomed to hearing the bells of the fire alarms on account of all the drills they made us go through. This was no fire alarm. It was the kind of sound that caused your hands to instinctively shoot up to your ears; a series of short harsh blasts like an air horn on a big truck. Mrs. Martin stiffened. Her eyes grew wide. Then she began shouting at us.

"All right children!" She shrieked. "Everyone line up at the door. Quickly now. Quickly!"

As soon as she was able to get her 30 scared-out-of-their-minds children in position, she yelled:

"OK, out in the hall now. Single file and no talking! Quickly now!"

Startled and frightened, I filed out of the classroom right on the heels of the kid in front of me. I remember how

84

strangely quiet it was. Even though the entire school—both teachers and students—were crowded into that same hallway, all I heard was the scuffling of tiny feet on the newly-waxed floor tiles. I think that was the first time I ever smelled fear.

It was 1962. The Cold War was raging. The entire world was still shaking from the terror of the Cuban Missile Crisis in which the two Superpowers brought us all to the very brink of nuclear war. Now the government wasn't taking any chances. Bomb shelters, canned food and "civil defense drills" were in every municipal building. Some people actually dug underground bomb shelters and stocked them with canned beans, tuna fish, and water jugs. They even held their own practice drills. It was a crazy, frightening time for all of us, but especially for us kids. Nightmares were as frequent as they were scary. Mine were no exception.

Of course, no one knew when bombs would fall. But if war did break out during school hours, the adults in charge were prepared. They had a plan. Their plan was called

Me and Danny

'duck and cover.' The instructions were very simple: students were to file out of the classroom, get close to the wall, duck down and cover their head. That was it. That was their plan.

I remembered how it felt to be doubled over in the hall, crouched next to Mary Jane Smith, my skinny knees touching my forehead, hands clasped on top of my crew cut—the wall tiles inches from my eyes—smooth like glass—pale yellow and clean—always clean. It was supposed to have saved us in the event of a thermonuclear war. No wonder we were all scared.

Of course, we never had an actual nuclear attack; but we held drill after drill, just in case.

As Dan and I stood inside the dark classroom waiting to summon up the courage to open the door, more memories came. I was in school marching in line with the rest of Mrs. Martin's class, idly dragging my fingertips across the smooth yellow tiles thinking how they reminded me of the yellow brick road in the *Wizard of Oz*.

Suddenly, a sharp sound shook the thoughts out of my head, returning me to the present. It was Danny. He was turning the knob of the classroom door.

Click!

The sound of the door latch echoed throughout the empty school hallway like Thor's mighty hammer, shocking me back to reality.

Danny and I shot each other a nervous glance. The door made a sound that could easily be heard throughout the whole school! He timidly pulled on the heavy classroom door until, like a bucket of cold water; the brightness of the hallway hit us full in the face. I squinted into the bright hallway and a shiver shot up my spine.

Danny and I were about to step out into the hallway of our old elementary school. On a Saturday. We were breaking the law. I hoped like heck nobody was there to catch us!

...Not So Awesome

Before stepping out from the dark classroom and into the bright hallway, Dan poked his head out to see if the coast was clear.

"Whaddya see? Anybody there?" I whispered.

"Nobody. Nobody here," he whispered back.

Slowly I followed Dan out into the empty hall. Sure enough, nobody there; just a bunch of desks and one of

those big mop-type custodian brooms—the ones you only
saw in schools and courthouses—leaning up against a
classroom bulletin board that was covered with blue
construction paper. Other than that, all we could see was the
long empty hallway that led to a set of double glass doors and
the bright summer day outside.

Again a memory visited me, that of gaining the
privilege of going out to clap erasers on the building's brick
wall just outside those double glass doors. How, if I stamped
the erasers in a circular pattern, they looked like flowers—
straight, white-chalk petals radiating out like a sunburst.

"Hey Mike," I heard Dan whisper. "You OK?"

"Oh," I said returning to reality. "Yep, whaddya
waiting for? Let's go."

We edged out into the hall little by little, gathering a
bit more courage with each tenuous step. As we tiptoed past
classrooms, my mind, and no doubt Dan's too traveled back
to the time when we were students there. Of course, back

Me and Danny

then it seemed like an eternity, as much as an eternity can seem to a 10-year-old.

We went past Mrs. Wermouth's room. Poor Mrs. Wermouth. For some reason her hairdo offended me. I guess it was my fledgling artistic sense or something. She just appeared kind of disheveled, like she was up too early or something; hadn't enough time to get ready.

So this one day, we were saying the Pledge of Allegiance, you know, while staring lovingly at the flag, when my eyes wandered away for a second and I caught a glimpse of her at the front of the room. She looked different. Then it dawned on me; she combed her hair! And being the sensitive child that I was, I thought it would be nice of me to recognize her efforts; it would make her proud.

So I did, congratulate her that is. Yeah, that was a mistake. Turns out sometimes grownups don't really like it when kids call them on something that maybe they'd just as soon we not notice. She wasn't mad or anything—she didn't forget about it either. In fact, I would be reminded of the incident whenever my parents came home from one of the open house evenings as well as all of our subsequent parent/teacher conferences.

The next room was Mrs. Martin's: she was a bear of a woman—tall, broad shoulders, deep voice. I liked her because she was always kind to us kids. She told us about a brother of hers who played professional basketball in Milwaukee. We cut her slack from that day on.

And finally past Mrs. Brach, whose intoxicating perfume made me ask for help when I didn't need it. And at whose hands I suffered the ultimate childhood humiliation: being spanked in front of the whole class for talking during story time.

Dan's voice:

"Whaddya wanna do?" he asked.

Convinced of being all alone in the school, we dispensed with the whispering.

91

Me and Danny

"I dunno. How about you?"

"I got it!" I said.

"What?"

"Let's go the gym. Shoot some baskets and maybe run around on some scooters!"

"Yeah! Let's go to the gym!"

The gym was back the other way, toward the classroom we had tumbled into 15 minutes before. It seemed to us now that no one was in the school. We had the place to ourselves! Our confidence put a bounce in our steps as we turned around and headed toward the gym.

"Oh, man. This is gonna be great!" Danny said.

"Yeah," I said. "Am I ever glad I decided to do this."

"What?" Danny said, his voice breaking a little. "Waddya mean **you** decided? Whose idea do you think this was, wise guy?"

"Mine of course," I said with a smile.

On the way to the gym, we walked past the main doors and the glassed-in foyer. It felt so strange to be inside looking out. Out there it was just another Saturday: guys going to the hardware store, cutting grass, cleaning out gutters and whatnot. And here we were inside a closed-for-the-weekend school! Everyone gone, no one here but us! Excitement mixed with tension, thrill with anxiety. We were having a ball playing "young hoodlums."

When we got to the gym we found it open. We headed right for the front where there was a little stage. In the back corner of this stage there was an area surrounded by steel fencing. This was the 'cage' where the gym teacher kept all his equipment. Among the basketballs, dodge balls and badminton rackets were the things I most wanted to fool around with: the scooters.

These foot-square hardwood platforms were on four shiny steel wheels which allowed them to move incredibly fast. They were used mainly for relay races—the

Me and Danny

activity everyone in class hoped we'd do—but I loved just cruising around on them. Boy, you could really fly.

Danny and I each got a scooter and proceeded to have the time of our lives. We whooped and hollered as we took turns shoving each other around that empty Saturday afternoon gym. Might sound silly, but it was wildly entertaining for us. It just felt, I don't know, sorta like freedom I guess. Gliding across that big, smooth-shellacked floor, wind in our faces, not a care in the world...

Next we took out a few dodge balls—those maroon-colored overblown jobs we used as weapons when we weren't playing kickball with them. After nailing each other a few times, we mostly just kicked them around the huge, empty gym.

Dan kicked one of them so hard it went clear to the ceiling where the big lights were housed in those round, steel cages. We sweated it for a quick second, hoping the light didn't break; it didn't. Our teachers never let us kids do things like this. But they weren't there. Maybe that's why it was so cool.

In the end we didn't hurt anything. Didn't want to. Afterall, this was our old school, where we'd gone every day for 4 years. We even put everything back where we found it when we had had enough.

"Man that was great!" I said somewhat breathless.

"Yeah. This is neat being in here doing whatever we want."

"Yeah. Hey waddya wanna do now?"

"I don't know. Wanna go see the offices?"

But before I could answer, we heard something: it stopped us dead in our tracks. It was the sound of keys jingling. And footsteps!

"Oh shoot!!" hissed Dan.

"What do we do," I said.

More keys jingling and more footsteps. And now whistling. We peeked around the corner and there, just

Me and Danny

walking into the offices was THE PRINCIPAL himself!

"Oh shoot!" Dan said again.

"Uh…we gotta get outta here, Dan!"

"Yeah. But how?"

There were no windows in the gym. We were stuck in a hallway just around the corner from the office. The only way out was right by the front of the main office, which would not have been a huge problem if it weren't for the fact that the walls of the main office were all glass, like a giant fish bowl!

"How we gonna get past the office?"

We were starting to sweat. We had been having so much fun. And now, it looked like we were in for it. I felt sick to my stomach.

"Dan, what are we gonna do?"

"We gotta make a run for it."

"What? Are you crazy? We'll never make it."

"Well what else are we gonna do? Can't stay here."

"We'll get caught. Never make it. He's gonna see us," I worried out loud.

Just then, we heard the keys again. This time they were coming our way! Oh jeez he was coming toward us! We had nowhere to hide and he was coming right for us! Dan looked at me. I looked at him. And then...there he was, Mr. Masterson! Walking right by us down the main hall! We held our breath. Maybe if we didn't move, he wouldn't look. Maybe if we didn't breathe...

But it was too late. As he was walking by the gym hallway, he glanced over and saw us.

He stopped short, grabbed his keys to silence them and just glared. We were paralyzed, shocked into immobility. Mr. Masterson looked stunned. And for a long moment, all three of us just stared at each other; with that deer-in-the-headlights look on our stunned faces. Was this really happening?

The next thing I knew the principal and I were both

Me and Danny

watching Danny sprint down the hall toward the exit. We stood there, Mr. Masterson and I standing shoulder to shoulder watching my best friend Danny as he pounded down the empty school hall, knees high, head down, running like there was no tomorrow. When he reached the end of the hall, he punched the glass doors open and disappeared into the bright Saturday afternoon.

I was speechless. He was too. And for a full minute Mr. Masterson—principal of Frank Knight Elementary School—and I, stood in silence, looking where Danny had been, like an old Road Runner/Wiley Coyote cartoon, leaving only a trail of dust and a plume of smoke behind.

He found his voice before I did.

"What is the meaning of this?" he blurted.

I hate it when grown-ups say that: "What is the meaning of this?" I never know what to say so I said nothing and just stared back at him.

"What are you doing in here?" he demanded.

"We were just looking around. Honest," I quavered. "We were just having a look around. You see, we used to go to school here and..."

I didn't get to finish. He was already moving toward the office with his hand reaching out as if to herd me like a goat heading for the barn.

"You come with me. And don't think you're going to run away like your friend there. Who is he by the way? Your friend?"

I didn't say anything.

"I said who is your friend. The one who ran away."

I said nothing. The sound of our footsteps echoed down the long hallway. I felt sick.

"Look, you are going to tell me your friend's name or I'm going to call your parents. Which is it going to be?"

He was coming out of his shock now and beginning to remember what he was doing and what had just happened. I imagine he'd just come in on his way to the hardware store to drop off some papers or something. He'd gotten lots more than he'd bargained for. And now he was mad. We had ruined his day off.

"I can't tell you," I finally said.

"What do you mean, you can't tell me?"

"I mean I won't tell you who he is"

"Why not? Why won't you tell me?" he asked as we rounded the corner to his office.

"Because I don't want to get him in trouble."

"Sit here." He pointed to a chair next to his desk. "Now let's get to the bottom of this." he said sternly.

"What's your name?"

"Michael."

"Michael what?" he asked while looking for some paper.

"Cerza."

"Michael Cerza. Michael, where do you live?"

He continued asking me questions until he got my

100

parents' names and my phone number. Then he asked me
again for Dan's name. I wouldn't give it to him.

"Do you realize that what you did is a crime? That
I could call the police and have you arrested?"

"I know. I'm sorry. We didn't mean any harm. We
were just looking around, that's all. We didn't hurt
anything."

"Well, we'll just see about that Michael."

And he took me by the arm and walked me down
the hall to the gym because that's where he saw us in the first
place. After being satisfied that we really hadn't caused any
damage, he marched me into every single classroom in the
school inspecting for damage. I was really sweating now.

By the time we got to the classroom that Danny and
I came in it seemed like days had passed since we tumbled
through that open window. Mr. Masterson opened the door
and we walked in. His eyes went straight to the window. It
was still open. In all the excitement and confusion, Danny

and I forgot to close the window. He had me!

"Is this where you came in?"

"Yeah, that's it."

He turned on the lights and walked around the room slowly looking at everything. He saw the wastebasket that Dan had kicked. It was upside down by the file cabinet.

"Did you do this?" he demanded.

"No."

"Well who did then?"

"I don't know," I said.

He frowned. He was looking for something to blame us for. And the fact that he was coming up empty obviously irked him.

"OK let's go," he said switching the lights off before escorting me out of the room.

"Michael, I'm going to call your parents now. And tell them what you've done. Is there anything you want to tell me before I do that?"

He wanted Dan's name. But I wasn't going to rat on my friend. No matter what he said or threatened.

"No."

"All right then, let's go." He herded me back to the office and into the hot seat again.

As I sat there listening to him dial my phone number, I tried to imagine what my mother was going to say. My Dad was at work at the furniture store so I knew I didn't have to worry about him...until later.

"Hello? Mrs. Cerza?"

His voice sounded different. Like everybody's voice does when they talk on the phone. Sometimes they raise it, sometimes they lower, depending on who they are talking with and what impression they want to give. The principal was using his lower than normal "official" voice now.

"Yes, this the principal over at Frank Knight School: Mr. Masterson. Yes, how are you today?"

Now he was just being sickening. I wished he'd just

103

get on with it.

"Yes, thank you, I am fine. Mrs. Cerza I'm afraid I have some bad news. No, no, it's not an injury. It's Michael. He...no no, he's all right. It's just that he is in trouble, Mrs. Cerza."

Although I was pretty far away from the receiver, I could hear my mom's voice. It was lower than usual too.

"Yes, I'm afraid he and a friend of his thought it was a good idea to break into the school this afternoon."

"Yes that's right. He and...well that's just it. I don't know the name of his friend. He won't tell me. He got away. That is, he ran away."

"Yes, I know it's upsetting, Mrs. Cerza. I don't have to tell you how serious this is Mrs. Cerza. I have to say...what's that? No. As far as I can tell, nothing was damaged. And nothing was...wait a minute please."

He put his hand over the phone and asked me to stand up.

"Empty your pockets please."

I did as he asked. I had a jackknife and a fireball in the left pocket.

"Now the other ones."

"I don't have anything else in my pockets." I said.

"Please empty them as I asked."

I dug into my empty pockets. I showed him my hands.

"Michael, did you or your friend take anything that didn't belong to you? Now tell the truth. You're in enough trouble as it is."

"No, we didn't take anything."

I told him the truth: neither Dan nor I took anything. We were just looking around. But before I could say that last part he broke in...

"No. Mrs. Cerza. Michael swears nothing was taken by him or his friend."

"No. This is not a small thing. I'm sorry to have to

call you about this. No, I do not plan to call the police, but you do realize that I could."

"You're welcome. But I do need to make sure that nothing was damaged or stolen. Yes I know I have looked but if anything turns up missing in the next week, I'm afraid I will have no choice but to call the police."

"Yes, that's right. Now Mrs. Cerza I am willing to let Michael go if I can have your word that you will try to get him to tell me who his friend was that broke into the school. Will you do that?"

I heard my mother answer that she would.

"All right then. Would you come and pick him up now?"

I knew what she'd say to that. My Dad had the car at work. She couldn't come get me.

"Oh. Well, your house is close by isn't it?"

"Well then I guess it would be all right if I just sent him home then."

106

Michael Cerza

"You're welcome. And Mrs. Cerza, I will be in touch later this week if anything is missing or damaged. Yes. You're welcome. Goodbye now."

He sounded so nice on the phone. It was sickening. After he hung up, he turned away from his desk, faced me. His face was stern, like stone. And with his most authoritarian, no-nonsense face, said:

"Michael, I hope you have learned your lesson. I hope you realize how serious this is. Now, I will give you one last chance to tell me who your friend was."

He paused. His eyes bored into mine, unblinking. He was trying his best to remain calm. I said nothing. Then, all of a sudden he snatched up his keys, rough-like and motioned for me to get up. It looked like he wanted to slap me or something. But he herded me back down the hall, toward the light of day. At the door he turned to me and said in an even monotone:

"I trust we won't be seeing you around here

107

anymore Michael. Goodbye."

I half-heartedly said "goodbye" and walked out into the afternoon sunlight. I was glad to be out. Real glad. But the gladness soon passed as I remembered what I was about to face. My mother. And then my father. I wondered where Dan got to after he sprinted out of the school. Was he worried about me…if I'd told on him or not and if Mr. Masterson was going to be calling his mom? It was a long slow, hot, walk back home.

I was happy to be out of that scrape, that's for sure. And I was glad I didn't squeal on Danny. But here's the thing—as I write about this harrowing childhood incident so many decades later…

You know how when something not so great happens to you and it's *so* not so great that you just as soon forget the whole thing…like it never happened? Well…I don't get it, but I can't for the life of me remember what took place after Mr. Masterson let me go. I mean, this was a big thing, or at least it could have been; it was breaking and entering, there are laws against such things. I could have been prosecuted, right? But still, I don't remember what my father said or what my mother said or even if I ever told my siblings. But this I'm sure of: Right or wrong, I never told anyone who was with me that summer day 60 years ago. I never told on my friend.

Riding Trees

Growing up in a small town had its advantages. For one thing, the crime rate was pretty darn low. The most common offense was something like a misguided teenager pocketing a magazine down at Crayton's drug store. Well that, and the odd rumors of bored youngsters—high on Ripple wine—tipping cows. This was a disturbing prank where a bunch of these amateur drunks would line up on one side of a poor unsuspecting dairy cow then push altogether until the docile creature falls over. Crazy, misguided small town amusement for sure. On the positive side, there definitely cool things about tiny town living.

For one thing, there was no traffic to speak of. In fact, traffic was so light, we could ride our bikes right down the middle of the noonday street without being in anyone's way. And if a body were to feel the necessity to cross the street between traffic lights, no one honked at them. Folks just being folks.

But...as I said before, finding things to do in this sleepy Upstate New York village was a horse of different color—at least for a kid too old to play on the swings and too young to drive. We had to be pretty creative not to die of boredom. And although Dan and I weren't exactly astronaut material back then, we felt like absolute rocket scientists when it came to thinking up things to occupy our time.

We kinda followed our noses through making do

111

Me and Danny

with what we had: driveway basketball, backyard golf, touch football, tree forts, cartoons, swimming, neighborhood games, breaking and entering...hardly exotic endeavors (with the exception of that last one of course).

You gotta remember, this was 1962; high-tech entertainment devices like frisbees, slinkies, and silly putty were just then becoming popular. And if we wanted a motorbike, we'd just clothespin a playing card onto the frame so it would set to fwapping against the spokes of the wheel as soon as you started pedaling; sounded just like one.

Naturally, we had bikes and roller skates, things like that, but snowboards and skateboards weren't being mass-produced yet so if we wanted to ride a skateboard, for example, we'd have to make one first, which we did.

Now to make a skateboard, we had to come up with two things: the board and the skates. First the board. This was the easy part. For the deck of our homemade skateboard we picked through whatever scraps of lumber

112

that happened to be lying around. It just had to be flat and with not too many nails in it. Next, the wheels.

For the wheels on our skateboard, we scavenged the wheels from another form of entertainment common back in the day: roller skating. Essentially, we just took the skates apart—front and rear wheels—and nailed them to the front and back of our scrap of lumber. Voila! A skateboard. Not exactly rocket science but close enough for a couple of Upstate New York 10-year-olds.

When we weren't playing backyard golf, marauding around on our 20-inch motorbikes, or cruising around on our fake skateboards, there was another outdoor activity we sort of invented; it involved the forest, some tall trees and a whole lot of dumb, youthful enthusiasm.

It came to us one day while we were smacking golf balls around in the field next to Frank Knight School. Dan had just shanked one off into the woods and now we were poking around with our clubs trying to find it.

Me and Danny

"What was it again?" I asked.

"A Dunlop 4. How many times do I have to tell you?"

"Hey don't yell at me. I'm not the one who lost it."

"And what difference does it make anyhow? It's not as if you're gonna find one and then *leave* it there if it's not the right one!"

He had a point. There weren't a whole lot of golf balls in these woods. And whatever balls we found were most likely ours anyway. We were the only ones hitting balls around in that field.

"Yeah whatever. Just keep looking. Was it a good one?"

"Brand new."

"No slices?"

"Nope."

"That sucks. We gotta find it."

We were about thirty yards apart, walking slowly,

swinging our clubs and poking weeds and branches looking
for something white and round. Then Danny called:

"Here it is!"

Those words. Those three words…perhaps the
sweetest sound in the world when you were looking for a lost
ball. "Here it is." What a triumph! What a relief! A lost ball
had been found! Beautiful, beautiful words.

"Where?" I called, tripping my way over to him.

"Here," he said.

Then,

"Oh forget it!"

"What…what's wrong?"

"Nothing, it's just another mushroom."

This happened all the time. We'd think we found it
only to get closer and see that it was one of those perfectly
round white mushrooms. Man, that was the worst. So close,
yet so far. Cruel, cruel nature.

We continued looking for another ten minutes then,

Me and Danny

"Forget it man. We're never gonna find it."

"Yeah. But I hate to lose that one."

"Yeah. I know. If this brush wasn't so thick, we might have a chance."

"Hey, wait a minute. I have an idea." I said.

"It's hard to see in all this bramble, right? But what if we were higher?"

"Higher?" Dan said incredulously.

"Yeah, higher." I answered, pointing up.

"You lost me. What the heck are you talking about?"

"What if we were up in there. In the trees?" I said.

"What? Are you kiddin' me?"

"C'mon. Let's try it. What the heck." I said.

"Right. You first. It's *your* idea," scoffed Dan.

"OK." I stood my club up against a big tree and looked around for just the right tree to climb.

"Hey, Tarzan. What about that one?" Dan said

pointing to a tall pine.

My eyes followed his finger a little ways into the heavy woods. There, behind an old stump and some pricker bushes I saw a tall pine.

"That the one?" I asked, pointing into the woods. "It's got nice limbs, kind of like a ladder almost."

"Yeah, that's it," Dan said.

We made our way over to the base of the tree, gingerly brushing aside the branches of the pricker bushes. When I reached the pine tree I grabbed hold of the limb closest to the ground. I was a good tree climber, so it didn't take long before I was twenty feet above the ground looking down at Danny. I situated myself in the crotch of one of the bigger limbs, anchored my feet and started scanning the forest floor below.

"See anything?" Danny yelled up at me.

"Naw," I grunted, reaching for another limb.

Just then, my left foot slipped. I jerked my free

117

hand up to the nearest limb; it caught on a jagged branch tearing a small patch of skin from the palm.

"Ow!" I hollered.

"You OK?" hollered Dan.

I reoriented myself on the branch, replanted my feet and drew my hand up to my eyes. It was just a scratch.

"Yeah, I'm fine."

I licked the blood off the wound and looked down at Danny. He was saying something to me, but I couldn't hear him.

"Hey do me favor willya?"

"What? What did you say?"

"Don't do anything stupid like fall. I don't want to have to carry you outta here."

"Don't worry, *Mom*. I got a good hold this time."

I didn't see anything that even looked like a golf ball from my spot in the tree so I climbed a little higher. But the other trees made it tough to see the ground; especially the

118

little saplings. They were all over the place. Tall and thin with heart-shaped leaves that turn yellow in the fall. They seemed to be the most popular tree in that part of the woods.

Then I got an idea.

"Hey Dan."

"What?"

"I just thought of something."

"What? Where the heck are you?"

"Right here. Above you."

"I can't see you. Where are you…Oh, never mind. I see you."

"I got a great idea. See those little trees?"

"Trees? You're kiddin' right? Which ones for cryin' out loud?" he said.

"Those trees. The tall…"

"What? I can't hear you," yelled Dan.

"I said do you see those tall trees?"

"Tall trees," he repeated, swiveling his head back

119

and forth.

"You mean the saplings?"

"Yeah, the saplings."

"Yeah…so? What about 'em?"

"Well what if…" I began.

"Hey."

"What if we…" I started again.

"Hey!" Danny yelled up at me.

"Why don't you come down outta there so I can hear you?"

"Yeah, Ok. But see those trees?" I said starting down.

"Yeah, yeah I see them. So what?"

I began climbing down out of the pine tree, being careful not to get the sap all over me. Nothing worse than pine tree sap. If it gets anywhere on you, your hands, your shirt, your legs, you might as well smear it all over you and call it cologne.

120

Michael Cerza

When I reached the bottom limb, I jumped down to the ground almost landing on top of Dan.

WUMP!

"Jeez!" he yelled. Waddya tryin' to do, kill me?"

"Sorry," I said a little absentmindedly.

I was too busy thinking about my great idea.

"OK." Said Dan impatiently. "What is this big idea of yours?"

"Well I got to thinking. These saplings. They're real tall and real skinny. I bet they bend like crazy. And I was thinking, being way up there just now. What if I was to reach out, grab a hold of one of them and let it take me down."

"What? Have you gone nuts 'er something?"

"No. Listen. This is how it'd work...I think anyway."

"First you pick out a tree. It'd have to be small enough to bend but not so small that it would break."

121

Me and Danny

"Yeah, then what?" Dan said with his hands on his hips like he always does when he doesn't believe me.

"Well, then you climb it and ride it down."

"Ride it down," Dan repeated. "Ride it down. You say you just ride it down. Down where?"

"Well to the ground you ninny…where else?" Now I was the one losing patience.

"Oh. But how? I mean how do you think that's gonna work? Won't the tree just break?" he asked as if I knew the answer.

"Nah! The tree won't break," I said with authority. At least I don't think it will," I said under my breath.

"Oh you **think**. Oh, that's good. You think," he echoed back. "And maybe this is one of the stupidest ideas you've ever had. Ever think of that?"

"C'mon, where's your sense of adventure? Let's try it. We'll pick a little one first, ok? C'mon Dan?"

"OK, OK. You first," he said flashing a thin smile.

"Jeez I never realized what a big baby you are." I said, returning his smile.

"Hey, who you callin' a big baby. I said all right didn't I? Then all right. Let's go."

Dan followed me deeper into the woods. My eyes darted back and forth looking for a glimpse of those green heart-shaped leaves. Then I saw them. They were about fifty feet from where we were standing. They were aspen all right, an entire stand of them, with their thin gray trunks, and heart-shaped leaves. And there were lots of them, made-to-order, perfect specimens for my tree riding experiment.

As we picked our way toward them over fallen limbs and blackberry bushes, I began making plans in my head: how to climb up the thin trunks without falling over, what to grab onto for support, how to launch myself out and down and from how high? I hoped this wasn't like Dan said: nothing more than the stupidest idea I ever had.

All Right, It's On!

As we approached the stand of aspens, I could feel my confidence evaporating like a parking lot puddle on a hot day. *Hmmmm,* I thought. *Tall trees. Thin trunks. What was I thinking?* I didn't want Dan to know.

"All right! Here we go!" I said, hiding my worry. "Look at these babies! Man this is gonna be great!"

124

"Hmmph," said Dan. "I can hardly wait."

I picked my way through the naked trunks trying to
avoid the vines that lay on the forest floor just waiting to trip
you up like one of those wise guys on a camping trip when
they're bored or just because they can, not that that ever
happened to me mind you.

Anyhow, I sized up each tree as I passed them,
running my eyes up their skinny trunks till the sun's glare
made me wince. I picked out a beauty, right in the middle of
the stand. It was straight and my goodness it was tall. It
seemed to go on forever, stretching way, way up, nearly
touching the blue sky above. There was only one problem:
the branches didn't sprout until about ten feet up the trunk:
way over our ten-year old heads.

It wasn't like the pine trees we were used to
climbing, with limbs sticking straight out from the trunk
every two feet or so. No ladder this time. No, if I wanted to
climb this baby, I'd have to shimmy all the way up until I

reached the first branch. And even if I did reach that first branch what if it wasn't strong enough to hold me? My mind was churning pretty good now. *What if I wasn't strong enough to hold me? What if I couldn't even make the first branch? What kind of excuses am I going to try to pitch to Dan if I chicken out?*

"Ok, Tarzan, waddya waiting for? Christmas?"

"Hey, you wanna go first?" I shot back.

"Wasn't *my* idea," he returned.

"Ok then don't rush me."

"Well if you're gonna chicken out, I'd like to know now. I got stuff to do."

He was being a real pain so I decided I'd be a pain right back. It'd kill some time…give me more time to figure out how the heck I was going to do this thing.

"Right. Man, you got nuthin' is what you got."

"Who you talking to? Why, I got more…"

I didn't let him finish. I knew that whatever he said would make more sense than what I had; which was nothing.

126

Just a crazy idea. Naturally, I played it up bigger.

"Oh will you look at Mr. Big Shot! What do YOU have to do? This your day to pick up the president or something?" I said in my best sarcastic whine.

"Aw forget it. I'm goin' home," he said as he turned away and started walking.

"OK, OK," I said quickly.

I pushed him too far. Dan and I knew each other well enough to know each other's limits. We never ever fought…well just that one time. But that's another story.

As he walked away, I decided to throw caution to the wind and go for it! Rooting my legs firmly to the ground, I drew a deep breath, reached up as high as I could, grabbed a handful of sapling and swung my legs up toward the trunk.

"Here I go. Look. I'm climbing. Look!"

I heard a rustle of leaves behind me. He was coming back.

By the time he got to the tree, my feet were even

Me and Danny

with his shoulders.

Climbing now, I was finding my rhythm: In quick spurts I shot my hands up and grabbed the thin trunk, then— almost at the same time—I slid both feet up the trunk and tried to anchor them long enough to repeat the cycle. First my hands then my feet, then my hands again, then my feet. I grunted with each fitful advance. It went more smoothly than I had imagined it would. And if it weren't for my wet sneaks slipping on the narrow trunk, it would have gone even better.

"Hey, you're doin it!" Dan exclaimed. "Keep goin'. Keep goin'."

I'd done it! After just a few minutes, I had managed to make it all the way up to where the first branches shot out from the trunk.

"Ugh!" I puffed. "I made it!"

"Great," he said. "Now what?"

I was clinging to the side of the tree like a

chimpanzee, the thin branches clutched in my ten-year old fists, the tiny trunk pinned between the soles of my P.F. Flyers. I was stuck. If I loosened either grip, I'd fall to the ground like a ripe peach.

"It's simple," I lied.

"All I need to do now is climb higher and…"

"Yeah? THEN what? Why don't you just come down so we can get home. It's getting dark for cryin' out loud."

I didn't answer. I was determined to do this. I figured, what the heck; I've made it this far. What's the worst that could happen?

Famous last words.

I reached up and got hold of a branch. I pulled myself up enough to get my foot on the branch my hand used to be on. Then I repeated the same motion. This brought me up another six or so feet. Then I realized something.

Me and Danny

I was running out of tree.

The trunk was disappearing, which is to say it was getting thinner and thinner. The weight of my body was causing the top of it to sway back and forth. Back and forth. My stomach felt like I was on a roller coaster; that kind of wishy-washy throw-up sick feeling we all love to hate.

Suddenly, I heard Dan's voice:

"Hey!" he screamed.

I heard a violent rustle of the leaves below me. Dan was running.

"Look out! You're falling!"

He was right. I was falling...or about to...from the top of a thirty-foot tree, in the middle of the woods, with no one around. *Maybe I should have thought this thing through a little further.*

"Grab something! Quick? Grab something! You're gonna fall!"

I had a strangle hold on the tiny trunk of the aspen

130

tree. I'd have to let go with one hand at least. Great idea. Except for one thing: I couldn't.

Time seemed to stop. My knuckles were white from the strain, my feet, jammed into the crotch of branches a few feet down from my hands were starting to hurt. Yet I remember thinking how beautiful it was way up there. The bright green of the aspen leaves, the way they shone vividly against the purplish late afternoon sky.

I glanced down to the ground below. It was a carpet of yellow and red leaves, just beautiful. It seemed like a long way down though; much farther down then it seemed looking up. It gave my stomach a queasy feeling. My midsection tightened and for a moment I felt like I had already fallen.

"Hey! Hey!" I heard Danny yell.

My mind seized on his voice and I was all at once back in my body. To my great relief, the tree stopped swaying. It was then that I truly realized that I was up a tree

131

without a ladder and that there was absolutely no way that Danny could help me. I was on my own, thirty feet up!

"Dan!" I heard myself scream. "What do I do? What do I do?"

Uh Oh!

"Hold on! Just hold on! Try not to move!"

I switched my hands on the skinny trunk trying to stay as still as possible. My feet were so tightly jammed together it was all I could do to stand the level of pain that was beginning to set in. *Man, I'm in trouble,* I thought.

"All right. I got it."

I looked down to where I thought Dan was. He wasn't there. I panicked.

Me and Danny

"Dan! Dan! Where are you?"

"Here. I'm over here!" he yelled.

"Where? I don't see you!" I screamed, starting to feel the panic rising inside me.

"Here. Look over here. To your right. Look to your right!"

I switched hands again, trying to position myself so I could move to my right. "Where? I don't see you!"

"Over here! Over here!" he yelled.

I still couldn't see him down below. My hands started to slip. I switched again, this time moving around to my left.

"Here! Look straight down! Straight down!"

"What? Straight down? You were on the right. You said on the right!" I yelled, with more panic now.

"Down. Just look down! But don't move! You're gonna fall!"

I tried to look down like Dan said. But a strange

thing happened. I was clinging to the top of this skinny tree, and the only thing that was keeping me there was the death grip I had on the tiny trunk. I realized that in order for me to look straight down, I had to move the whole top part of my body to one side or another, a dicey proposition to be sure. And the stakes were high; if I moved too much, the thin trunk I had a hold on would sway big time and I'd fall like a stone.

I moved my head first, looking over my left shoulder. The whole tree shifted suddenly to the left. My stomach did somersaults. I jerked myself back upright.

"That's it! Look down!" Danny yelled.

"I can't! I'll fall!" I yelled back.

Silence.

I tried to collect myself enough to think clearly. I have to do something. I can't stay up here all night. How the heck could I stay up here? Of course not. I have to figure out how to get down…without killing myself.

Me and Danny

My hands were beginning to feel numb. My feet hurt like heck. My stomach was doing cartwheels.

"C'mon, Mike. You gotta get down from there. Try climbing down!"

Amazingly that was the one thing that I had not thought of...*climb down the same way I climbed up. Of course!*

"OK. Here goes!" I yelled.

I slowly started to peel back the fingers of my left hand. When they were free but were still gripping the tree lightly, I started working on my right hand. Finally I could feel them again. *This was it*, I thought. *I gotta make a move, as much as I don't want to.*

I released the tree with my right hand and moved it carefully below a branch near my waist and tightened my grasp. Next, I took my left hand and did the same thing. *So far so good*, I thought.

Next came my feet. I had to move my feet somehow. But how? I could hardly feel them now they'd

136

been stuck in the crotch of the branches so long. I moved the toes of my top foot first, then the toes of the foot that was jammed underneath it. My hands were starting to go numb again so I tried flexing them on and off.

I gotta make a move here pretty fast, I thought. *No more pussyfooting around. All right.... Here goes.*

I yanked up on my top foot. To my surprise it came up much faster than I thought it would, sending my knee crashing up into the branch above it.

"Ow!" I yelled. My body jerked to one side.

"Look out!" I heard from below.

Before I knew it, the tree jerked violently to one side and I was falling! My hands were still gripping the slender tree, my feet dangling below me. Falling...falling! It all happened so suddenly, and I was moving so rapidly... but somehow it seemed like it was all in slow motion. Blurred streaks of green and yellow in my vision, the sound of branches bending, then snapping...and Danny screaming up

137

Me and Danny

at me the whole way down. It was truly a wild scene. I remember being somehow aware of the excitement and the terror together, as if they were somehow the same thing—my fluttering stomach, my reeling thoughts, the thrill of flying through the fresh, afternoon air, all the while waiting to see if I was going to get hurt when it was all over.

It seemed to take a long time but really it probably wasn't. It was all over in less than 20 seconds I bet. I landed with a dull thud. My legs were scraped and my hands and arms bloody but other than that...I'd survived pretty well intact.

"You OK?" Danny said, running over to me.

"Yeah. I think so."

"Man, that was a close one. I was beginning to think about running for the fire department or something."

"Yeah, or the ambulance," I said.

"You sure you're ok?"

"Yeah. Just my knees and my hands. I don't know. I

guess I was pretty lucky."

"I'd say you were REAL lucky. Whatever possessed you to do that?"

"Man, I don't know. I guess I learned my lesson."

"Good," Dan said, obviously relieved.

As we made our way out of the woods and started the walk home, Dan turned to me:

"So what do you think? Would you ever do that again?"

"Not in your life," I said.

"So…this weekend then?"

"You bet!"

The Big Adventure

We planned our Big Adventure for the middle of the Upstate New York winter. We figured it this way; the blinding snow and biting North winds would drive us to the very brink of our endurance. And by doing this we might discover that we too, were Superheroes; able to leap tall

Michael Cerza

buildings in a single bound, bend steel with our bare hands, stuff like that. Just in case though, we went ahead and threw some stuff into a plastic bag, this was years before backpacks became a thing; back when the only people who wore them were boy scouts, soldiers, and astronauts. Danny brought the baloney sandwiches while I supplied the peanut butter sandwiches and candy bars. We each brought a few comic books, for Superhero inspiration, and a pocketknife, just because we were boys I suppose.

The big day dawned gray and cold. It had snowed the day before and the dark skies meant snow was a strong possibility today as well. Dan and I dressed for the cold like we were going sledding or skating out on the lake: two pair of jeans over long-johns, two sweatshirts over t-shirts, heavy pack-boots with two pair of socks and plastic bread bags stuffed inside, just in case our boots leaked—which they did all the time. So off we went, looking like a couple of big ole grey marshmallows shuffling across town. We headed toward

141

Me and Danny

the old Sylvania Industrial Plant where we'd pick up the railroad tracks: our path out of civilization. As we crossed the tracks we said our last goodbyes to our little village, warms beds, and electricity. Shortly we came to the first railroad signal. We turned left with the tracks and set to following the snow-filled path between the steel rails toward our big adventure.

We walked...and walked...and walked. Our heavy boots trudged through the deep December snowdrifts covering the railroad tracks making high pitched squeaking noises with each strenuous stride. I don't remember ever walking so much, for so long, through such icy winds...having so much fun. We talked as we went. About the things that mattered to us: school, other kids, our brothers and sisters, and the presents we were hoping to get when Christmas came the following week.

After a few hours our stomachs let us know it was time to make camp. So we broke off the tracks and headed for a hedgerow a little ways down from where we were walking. The going got slower and slower the farther we strayed from the tracks.

Step by laborious step we made our way toward the hedgerow, our boots getting periodically stuck in the ever-deepening snow. At the same time, the underbrush we encountered became thicker and thicker. After a few minutes of struggling, Danny and I came to a particularly nasty patch of raspberry bushes. The thorns ripped and tore at our coat sleeves as we fought our way through. Finally, we broke through. What we found on the other side of this tortuous path was as unexpected as it was wondrous.

A winter paradise lay before us; a sweeping panorama of pristine winter beauty stretching from where we stood, down and across an immense valley of newly fallen snow. The vast field swept left to right across the land from hedgerow to hedgerow, rising at its outer boundaries. The contrast between our experience tramping through the spiky

143

Me and Danny

brambles and this sudden open vista took our breath away.

It was so absolutely white and undisturbed it gave us the feeling we were on a Hollywood movie set rather than just some farmer's lower forty. Everything was soft and quiet; having none of the harshness we had endured all morning. The cottony snow blanketed the rolling hills folding gently at the edges of a narrow flowing brook. The branches of the bare trees were delicately outlined in white and bent gracefully down from trunk to earth. Squirrels scurried along them, like little four-legged acrobats, knocking fluffs of snow into the air as they went. It was so still we could hear the silence pounding in our ears. And though we were only ten, we could feel a certain spiritual calm in that sunlit wonderland. If magic was possible anywhere, we thought, it was possible here.

Four sandwiches, two Clark bars and several snow angels later, we left this beautiful spot and hit out once again for parts unknown. Following a small stream, we soon came upon a large open field. A barbed wire fence stopped us from going farther. A barbed wire fence? This far out? I mean we hadn't seen any sign of civilization since we split off from the railroad tracks hours ago. This was a head-scratcher. The hilly terrain made it impossible for us to see past the upper ridge, so we weren't sure what to do…turn around or push onward. But we were on a big adventure and in an exploring mood, so we gingerly hopped the barbed wire fence and headed up the snow-covered slope, excited to see what was on the other side. Our excitement for the unknown paid off sooner than we had imagined, for as we crested the hill, we saw that we weren't alone anymore.

The Chase

Scattered about this lonely, backwoods field was the biggest herd of cattle I ever saw. They were just standing there, staring...like we had stumbled on a secret meeting, and now they were waiting for the password. Heavy plumes of white water vapor puffed out of their cud-chewing mouths with every exhale. I never realized just how HUGE cows

146

really are up close. But there they were—bigger than life, twice as real and not ten feet away!

My mind felt the confusion of a million thoughts colliding. Time froze. Danny and I swapped startled stares. Like deer held motionless in the blinding glare of oncoming headlights we stood stock-still...face to face...in the frigid early afternoon air.

If this were an episode in one of our comic books the heroes of the story, Danny and I, would suddenly shed our human forms and emerge as...THE FEARLESS SNOW WARRIORS; TRIUMPHANT RULERS OF THE INVADING HORDE OF INTERDIMENSIONAL FARM ANIMALS!

But alas, we were not in a comic book; this was real life and we were standing there staring at a herd of cows in a cold snow-covered field less than a cars-length away armed only with a plastic bag, a peanut butter sandwich and a pocketknife.

147

Me and Danny

We stood there. Danny, me, and the cows…doing nothing. No sound, no movement. Just stood there staring. All of a sudden one cow raised a hoof and stomped it back down. Another stomped the ground, then another, and another. The next thing we knew, the tense silence was shattered by the sound of a zillion hooves thumping the frozen field. They were charging us! Funny thing, I don't remember turning around, but we sure must've. Because almost at the same time the cows startled into action, Danny and I were already pounding our way back through the snowy pasture, making a beeline to the barbed wire fence. We may have had comic book characters in *our* minds but these cows surely did not. They knew one thing: *GET THOSE LITTLE HUMANS!*

Thundering hooves. Right behind us. A million of them. A locomotive running us down. Louder and louder. Closer and closer. They were gaining on us!

These things are huge! How the heck could they be running

148

this fast? I wondered.

One of two things is going to happen: they catch up to us and trample our ten-year-old bodies into the snow, or we stumble into the barbed wire and get cut to smithereens. Danny and I ran as fast as our little legs could carry us. Huff, huff, huff, huff went our breathing; huff, huff, huff, huff went theirs. We could hear them closing in on us. How could this be happening?

We could see the barbed wire fence coming closer. But so was the herd. We sprinted down the hill, dodging fallen branches and frozen cowpies. When we finally reached the fence, we scrambled right over the top of it, miraculously avoiding getting snagged by the rusted wire.

Once over, we didn't stop to look behind us. Would they still be chasing us? Could they be? Danny and I weren't about to wait around to find out. Once we cleared the barbed-wire fence we didn't stop; we kept running, our feet caked with heavy snow, our lungs burning with the cold air. We kept on running, likety-split, out of the pasture, over the

Me and Danny

fence, straight into the next woods…screaming the whole way. We finally stopped when we didn't hear their hooves anymore. Dan and I stood there looking at each other, our chests heaving with the exertion of having outrun the cows. After a full minute we started to catch our breath enough to talk.

"Holy cow!" I said, still barely able to talk.

"You said it!" Danny barked.

"What the heck was **that?**" I said.

"Sheesh!...I don't know. But I'll never, **ever** look at another cow the same way lemme tell you. Man, they're scary!"

The whole episode, being so bizarre—just plain weird—could certainly have been an episode out of one of our Saturday morning cartoons, except it wasn't. It was real, and so was the terror. It scared the bejingles out of us!

Lost in the Woods

Getting pushed around by a bunch of angry cows left Danny and me feeling a little peckish so we raided our bags for something to eat. Slim pickings is what we found. Half a Snickers bar and one peanut butter sandwich (made from that weird bread that Danny's parents liked, the kind without the crusts). We ate the Snickers and slipped the sandwich into my bag, just in case we needed it later.

151

Me and Danny

You know, a winter's day in Upstate is a peculiar thing. For one thing, they're mighty short. It seems no sooner it dawns, than its bright white light turns gray and weak. Darkness falls like a heavy black curtain, sudden and complete. Then the *real* cold sets in. It was getting late; Danny and I were beginning to feel the cold, and we were dog-tired. We needed to find the railroad tracks...and soon.

"Ok, remind me never to go on another one of these adventures again. That was too close," Dan said over his shoulder to me.

"I'm right with you there. I didn't know cows hated people so much."

"I know. What did we do? We were just walking through the field," Dan said.

"Well, maybe that's what it was," I said.

"What? That's what what was?" he asked.

"Wait up will ya...lemme catch up. I can't hear you," I said.

152

Danny stopped walking for a moment and waited for me to catch up to him.

"Ok. Now. What is what we did?" Dan asked with exasperation.

"Hold on," I said motioning ahead of us with my mittened hand.

"Hold on for what?" Danny said, his voice breaking a little, a sure sign he was getting more and more annoyed with the whole situation.

"Just hold on…wait," I said quietly.

"What are you talking about?" he said loudly.

"Shhh! Not so loud."

"Why are you shushing me? We're out in the middle of nowhere," Dan said in full-blown irritation now.

"I know. That's my point," I said almost whispering.

"Mike, you're starting to freak me out. What are you talking about? We gotta get outa here. I'm cold and I

153

don't…."

"I know," I said, cutting him off.

"I'm not sure which way to go. I don't know where we are."

"Yeah, no kidding Sherlock. That's what I'm trying to say," he sputtered.

"Listen. Just listen will ya?" I said.

"For what?"

"Exactly," I said.

"What on earth are you talking about?"

"If you'd shut up for a minute…" I said, matching his exasperation.

"OK, this is how I figure it," I said in a low voice. "If we try to listen real quiet like, we might hear something that would give us a clue to where we are."

"OK, but do we have to stop walking? I mean this could take all day, and I don't want to be the one to break it to you, but we don't exactly have all day!"

●

"All right, all right, walk," I said in a hissing whisper.

"But be quiet for cryin' out loud. And keep your ears open! Can you do that? Please?"

"All right, all right. You don't have to yell," Danny said.

Danny and I slogged through knee-deep drifts of newly fallen snow for a few minutes, alone with our thoughts, trying not to think too much about how much trouble we could be in if we were really lost.

Just then we came upon what appeared to be a path. It ran from the field through which we were traipsing to a nearby patch of woods. It might be a path but we still had no idea where we were. Taking this path we realized, could either get us home, or get us hopelessly lost. It was getting colder by the minute, so we decided to take a chance...we took the path.

At first the path seemed easy and well-marked but

the farther we hiked the more dense the forest became until suddenly the lights went out, the path ended and we were lost! From our Boy Scout training we remembered that the best thing to do when you were lost was to remain calm and think things out.

So naturally we screamed wildly instead:

"Help!! Help!! Can anybody hear us? Help!!"

…then we stopped….and screamed again…

"Help! Help!!"

Then we stopped. And sure enough, during that moment of panic stricken quiet, a most glorious sound came to our ears: it was the sound of automobile tires running on pavement. We had stumbled upon a road!

"You hear that? Do you?" I yelled to Danny.

"I sure do," he said.

"We made it! We found a road!" I screamed.

"OK, OK, but which one is it?" Dan replied.

"I don't know but my money is on Black Brook."

156

"Old Black Brook Road! Yeah, I bet you're right. Man, this is great. We'll be home before you can say Great Krypton!" Dan yelled.

Help!

Old Black Brook Road is a lonely stretch of country lane traveled mostly by honest grubby farmers on their slow dinosaur-like machines. Among the broken-down houses that were scattered along this badly paved back road lived several of the town's more "colorful" folks.

Of all the strange characters on Old Black Brook

Road the Russos took the cake. Whenever my friend Danny and I went on one of our long bike rides, we always made a point of saving enough energy to sprint past the Russos. This was no easy thing because their property was huge. It was a test of endurance to pump our little 20-inch bikes fast enough to avoid the wicked jaws of their German Shepard dogs. The few times we didn't make it still provide a moment of reflected horror when revisited in my mind.

But the dogs were only part of the danger one encountered going past the Russo's place. The Russos themselves were terrifying. They were giants! Each of the three brothers stood about eight feet tall and bulged out about the same distance. With heavy black beards and small menacing eyes, they had only to come to the end of their driveway and look your way to make you ride right off the road, down the ditch and into the woods!

Naturally none of these thoughts came to our minds as we finally broke out of that dense pine forest. We were much too busy trying to figure out how we were going to get across the raging stream that separated us from the road home, dry socks, and warm food. Being wider than either of us could jump and gushing so fast that we probably wouldn't have the guts to try anyway, we decided on another strategy: we would build a bridge.

Some Serious Danger

So, gathering what we could in the way of materials, dead tree limbs and small saplings, we set upon the arduous task of building a bridge. Our little fingers were numb by the time we set the last pole in place. Danny and I stood next to the monstrosity we just piled up. Silence. Somebody had to be the one to try crossing this heap of junk. I spoke first.

"Uh…well, whaddya think? Will it work?"

"Darned if I know. Looks like just a pile of trash to me. Not sure if it's safe to cross."

"Yeah," I said. "Well, whaddya think?"

161

Me and Danny

"Mike, you just asked me that…and for your information, I still don't know. Looks like a pile of trash to me."

"Now who's repeating themselves?" I said. "Should we give it a try?"

"Well, we built the thing for a reason…it's getting dark and I'm getting really cold," Dan said.

"Yeah, me too. We've been out here forever."

Looking back on it I'm not at all sure how the job of crossing this heap of litter fell to Danny…maybe we drew straws or maybe we played a quick game of rocks and scissors. I don't know. But regardless of the method, it turned out to be a very important decision.

Danny took a few steps toward the 'bridge.'

"Hey, whaddya doin?" I asked.

"Well, somebody's gotta do it. Looks like I'm it."

And with that, Danny put one foot on the pile of

limbs. His foot slipped off immediately. The rush of the fast-moving stream caught his boot and threw him violently, straight up into the air. It all happened in slow motion. His body seemed to get stuck in the air, splayed out in all directions, then suddenly it came loose and plunged headfirst into the turbulent water below!

"Help! Help me...Mike!" he screamed.

Just a moment ago we were standing knee-deep in snow next to this torrent of water talking and now all of a sudden Danny was being swept downstream! It happened so quickly and with such violence that I found myself frozen in my tracks. He was quickly being carried out of sight. *What do I do? What do I do?*

Thoughts in my mind moved just as fast as Danny was disappearing and before I knew what was happening, I was running along the side of the streambed trying to keep up with him. Danny was being tumbled along with huge chunks of ice, broken limbs and rocks. I ran. Dodging bushes and trees I tried desperately to figure a way out of this horrible nightmare! Jumbled, disconnected thoughts swirled around in my mind like the murky brown water I was racing right next to.

'I'm only 10!...', I thought.   *'I couldn't possibly be in this serious a situation...it can't be real...it can't!'*

Then I saw it. Out of the corner of my eye. I rushed forward, pushing dried stalks of goldenrod aside as I ran. Just then, one snapped back right into my face.

"UGH!" I barked.

I brushed my face off with my dirty mitten. Then, looking up I saw it again. A bridge!..a real bridge!

I ran faster. The stream was raging now, carrying all sorts of dangerous debris with it. My mind raced.

'Danny's in serious trouble,' I thought. *'Go faster, go faster!'*

The bridge was getting closer. I ran faster. Now I felt something slipping. It was the plastic bag around my

164

shoulder. It was coming loose. Just then a sharp branch brushed my arm nearly causing me to fall. I caught myself. The bag was gone; so was our last sandwich.

Only a few feet now. The bridge was only a short distance away. I had to get there before the current swept Danny beyond under it; if I didn't, he'd be lost for sure. I had to run faster!

What happened next can only be explained this way:

In my mind, I became Ben, the giant of the Fantastic Four, the superhero. I—that is to say Ben the superhero, comic book star of the Fantastic Four—ran to the bridge ahead of Danny, climbed up into the trusses under the bridge and somehow braced myself as best I could in order to reach him. It must have been superhuman powers, because just as I wedged myself into the framework of the bridge, Danny came bobbing by underneath me.

"**Uh!... Uh!... Uh!**" I sputtered as I shot my arm down from the bridge. Our outstretched arms linked, and the force nearly pulled me into the stream with him. "**Gotcha!**" I blurted out. "**Hold on! Hold on!**"

"**Ah! Uh! Ugh!**" he barked in a low, rough-sounding voice. I felt his hand gripping my arm with all his might.

"**Oh! Oh! Oh! Hold onto me! Grab ahold!**" Danny yelled.

We were able to hold on to each other long enough to get a better grip and I slowly pulled his soaking wet body up and onto the bridge. He was safe!

We must have been quite a sight. Danny on top of me soaking wet, hair slicked down, body dripping gray icy water, face gripped with terror. And me, wet, filthy, breathing like a freight train, equally terrorized.

"Thanks, Mike. Thanks for saving me. I don't know what would've…"

"Yeah, I know," I said in gulps. "I know."

Home Again

It was a long, cold walk home, with lots of deep words exchanged between our chattering teeth. We were tired, cold, and humbled by the events of the day. Our adventure was more than we bargained for but in our hearts we were glad. Because as we approached the Russo's compound, we were not afraid...not one bit. We marched right past the house without so much as a thought to the dogs or the giants. We had done a lot of growing up that day.

Epilogue

During the years that followed, Danny and I shared many more boyhood adventures. But not long afterwards, things began to change.

I don't know how it happened or even why, but as high school approached, Danny and I drifted apart. His brother Charlie moved away, our Par-Three Course's tin cans filled in with dirt and worms. Cartoons gave way to Saturday morning baseball practice. We discovered girls.

Soon he became just another face in a crowded high school hallway.

Michael Cerza

Made in United States
North Haven, CT
04 October 2022